Mama D's Pasta & Pizza

by Giovanna D'Agostino

 Golden Press • New York

Western Publishing Company, Inc.
Racine, Wisconsin

Art Director: Remo Cosentino
Designer: Elizabeth Alexander
Cover Photography: Victor Scocozza
Illustrations: Ray Skibinsky

Printed in the U.S.A. by Western Publishing Company, Inc.
Published by Golden Press, New York, New York.

Library of Congress Catalog Card Number: 77-95314

Golden* and Golden Press* are trademarks of
Western Publishing Company, Inc.

Contents

About Pasta & Pizza

Rules are made to be broken, and there's one rule about pasta I'd like to break straight off. I disagree with those gourmets who say that every pasta should be served with certain sauces and no others. Sure, you can't serve tortellini in a heavy meat sauce. They'd drown, poor things. A large pasta needs a robust sauce, or the sauce is lost. But good sense tells you this. So don't worry about the rules, just use your head.

Most Italians like their pasta al dente, which means just, but just, chewable. But maybe you like it a little softer. So serve it softer. You only need two things to cook pasta right: a big pot and lots of water. Don't stint on either. Use a 6- to 8-quart pot, and fill it with water — at least 4 quarts of water for every pound of pasta, and more is better. For every 4 quarts of water, add 1 tablespoon of salt. Now, when you have the water at a rolling boil, throw the pasta in and stir it. Push up from the bottom so the strands are always moving and all separated and swirling around. Take a piece and bite into it. When you like the way it chews, drain and serve it.

As you become more familiar with pasta, you'll find that cooking times vary from brand to brand and even from homemade to homemade. Generally, I find that commercial pasta cooks in less time than that given on the box. Timing for homemade pasta varies tremendously depending on the thickness of the pasta. Very, very thin pasta takes seconds. Stuffed pasta takes longer, but it tells you when it's done: the pasta rises to the top of the pot. At the restaurant, I cook my pasta almost like rice. After 6 or 7 minutes, I turn it off. I don't just let it stand there. I stir it around from time to time, and after about 7 minutes it's cooked.

One reason for doing this book is to keep your hands from reaching automatically for the box of spaghetti on the supermarket shelf. There are so many different pastas that I couldn't mention them all. But most of all, I want you to have the pleasure of making your own pasta and pizza. It isn't hard and it isn't time consuming. If you haven't made pasta before, start with the step-by-step recipe on page 6. You'll find the smaller amount easier to handle.

As for pizza, it's almost impossible to ruin bread dough (and that's what pizza dough really is) unless the yeast is too old or you kill it with hot water. Check the expiration date on the package of yeast. The water you dissolve it in should register between 105 and 115 degrees. No thermometer? Just remember the water should be warm, not hot, and you'll be all right.

So don't be afraid. Plunge in and enjoy yourself. That's what life's all about.

Giovanna D'Agostino

Basic Pasta Dough

3 cups all-purpose flour	3 tablespoons oil
¾ teaspoon salt	6 to 9 tablespoons water
3 eggs	

Put the flour and salt into a large mixing bowl and stir to combine. Make a well in the center of the flour and add the eggs and oil. Using a fork, whisk the eggs with the oil until combined. Gradually begin to whisk in the flour from the side of the well. When the flour has all been worked in, the mixture will be crumbly.

Still using the fork, begin to add the water, 1 tablespoon at a time. Work well after each addition to incorporate the water into the mixture. Add only enough water to form the dough into a somewhat crumbly ball with your hand.

Transfer the dough to a lightly floured formica or wood surface and begin working it with the heel of your hand, pushing the dough away from you. If the dough is sticky, add more flour to the surface. Continue working the dough for about 10 minutes or until you have a smooth, elastic ball. Invert the mixing bowl and allow the dough to rest under it for 10 minutes. The dough is now ready to be rolled out and cut into shapes for desired pasta (see pages 7-11).

When rolling out the dough, always push in the direction away from the center of the dough. To maintain its shape and thin it evenly, rotate the dough frequently: rectangular and square sheets, ¼ turn; circles, ¼ turn at first, less as the dough gets thinner. Keep unrolled portion of the dough covered by the bowl.

Makes about: 1½ pounds noodles; 45 agnolotti; 24 canelloni; 156 cappelletti; 36 manicotti; 144 tortellini; 75 ravioli.

■ If this is your first try at making pasta, follow the step-by-step directions on page 6 to make ½ pound dough. You'll find the lesser amount easier to handle until you are more experienced.

> **The cooking times for homemade pastas vary with the thickness of the dough, but all cook faster than the commercial pastas.**

Step-by-Step Basic Pasta Dough

1. Put 1 cup all-purpose flour and ¼ teaspoon salt in a large mixing bowl. Stir with a fork to combine. Form a well in the center of the flour. Add 1 egg and 1 tablespoon oil to the well and whisk to combine.

2. Gradually begin to whisk in the flour with the fork from the side of the well. Toward the end, you will have to stir it in. The mixture will be crumbly. Add 1 tablespoon water, sprinkling it over the dough.

3. Mix well with the fork to incorporate all the water. Add up to 2 tablespoons more water, but only enough to form the dough into a rough ball with your hand. It will be far from perfect in shape.

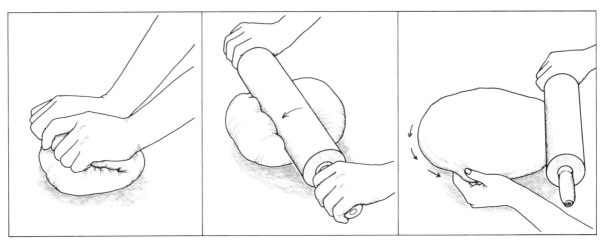

4. Work the dough on a lightly floured formica or wood surface, pushing it with the heel of your hand. Treat it roughly and work it for about 10 minutes or until the dough forms an elastic, smooth ball.

5. Cover and rest the dough for about 10 minutes. Check the instructions (pages 7-11) for the pasta you want to make and begin rolling out the dough on a lightly floured surface. Roll from the center of the dough.

6. Rolling always from the center and away from yourself, rotate the dough frequently to maintain its shape: Rectangular and square sheets, ¼ turn; circular ones, ¼ at first, a little less with each roll.

Basic Pasta Dough Variations

Whole Wheat Pasta Dough
Using 1 cup all-purpose flour and 2 cups whole wheat flour, follow the recipe for Basic Pasta Dough (page 5).

Semolina Pasta Dough
Using 2 cups all-purpose flour and 1 cup semolina, follow the recipe for Basic Pasta Dough (page 5).

Green Pasta Dough
Add 6 tablespoons cooked, pureed and well-drained spinach to the flour mixture along with the eggs and oil in the Basic Pasta Dough (page 5). The same can also be done with whole wheat or semolina pasta dough.

> **Semolina is made from durum wheat and is available only in stores carrying Italian foods.**

Preparing, Cooking and Serving Homemade Pasta

Cannelloni
Divide the dough into 6 parts. Roll each part into a 9- to 10-inch square (the thinner, the better). Divide each square into 4 smaller squares. Cook in a 6- to 8-quart pot of boiling salted water for about 3 minutes. Remove to a colander and run under cold water. Drain on a clean towel.

Place 2 tablespoons filling (see pages 12-13) on each square and roll up. Put seam side down in a baking pan. Add about ¼ inch of hot water to the pan and cover the cannelloni with 2 cups of your favorite tomato sauce (pages 15-20). Sprinkle with grated Romano cheese.

Cover firmly with aluminum foil and bake in a preheated 375° oven for 1 hour. Remove the foil and sprinkle with ½ cup mozzarella cheese. Bake uncovered for 10 minutes more or until the cheese is melted. If desired, serve topped with additional sauce.

Lasagne
Divide the dough into 3 parts and roll out on a lightly floured board into sheets about 12 inches square. Cut each square into six 2-inch strips.

Cook in a 6- to 8-quart pot of boiling salted water for about 3 minutes. Drain and put into cold water. (See pages 26-27 for lasagne recipes, or use fillings on 12-13).

■ You can vary the length of the lasagne strips to fit any pan you want to use.

Cappelletti

Divide the dough into 6 parts and roll out on a lightly floured board into 9-inch squares. Divide into 1½-inch squares (5 equally spaced vertical and horizontal cuts).

Place ¼ teaspoonful of filling (see pages 12-13) in each square. Fold diagonally to form a triangle. Seal the edges. Holding the folded side of the triangle against your finger, bring the two bottom points of the triangle around your finger and pinch together to form a little cap.

Cook in a 6- to 8-quart pot of boiling salted water for about 6 minutes and serve with your favorite sauce (pages 15-20). You can also cook and serve cappelletti in beef or chicken broth.

Tortellini

Divide the dough into 2 or 3 parts and roll out as thinly as possible into sheets. Cut into 1½-inch circles. Place ¼ teaspoonful of filling (pages 12-13) in each circle and fold over to form a half circle. Seal the edges. Holding the folded side of the dough against your finger, stretch the two points of the dough around it to form a coronet, or small crown. Pinch the ends together.

Cook in a 6- to 8-quart pot of boiling salted water for about 6 minutes and serve with your favorite sauce (pages 15-20). You can also cook and serve tortellini in chicken or beef broth.

■ Cut leftover dough into small shapes. Put into a covered container and keep for soups.

Manicotti

Divide the dough into 6 equal parts and roll out on a lightly floured board into sheets about 9x10 inches. Cut in half across the 9-inch width and cut each half into 3 equal strips.

Manicotti are sold as large tubes for stuffing, but they're better if you make them yourself.

Cook in a 6- to 8-quart pot of boiling salted water for about 3 minutes. Remove to a colander and run under cold water. Drain on a clean towel.

Place 2 tablespoons filling (see pages 12-13) on each strip and roll up from the long side. Put seam side down in a baking pan. Add about ¼ inch of hot water to the pan and cover the manicotti with 2 cups of your favorite tomato sauce (pages 15-20). Sprinkle with grated Romano cheese.

Cover firmly with aluminum foil and bake in a preheated 375° oven for 1 hour. Remove the foil and sprinkle with ½ cup mozzarella cheese. Bake uncovered for 10 minutes more or until the cheese is melted. If desired, serve topped with additional sauce.

Cappelletti

Tortellini

Manicotti

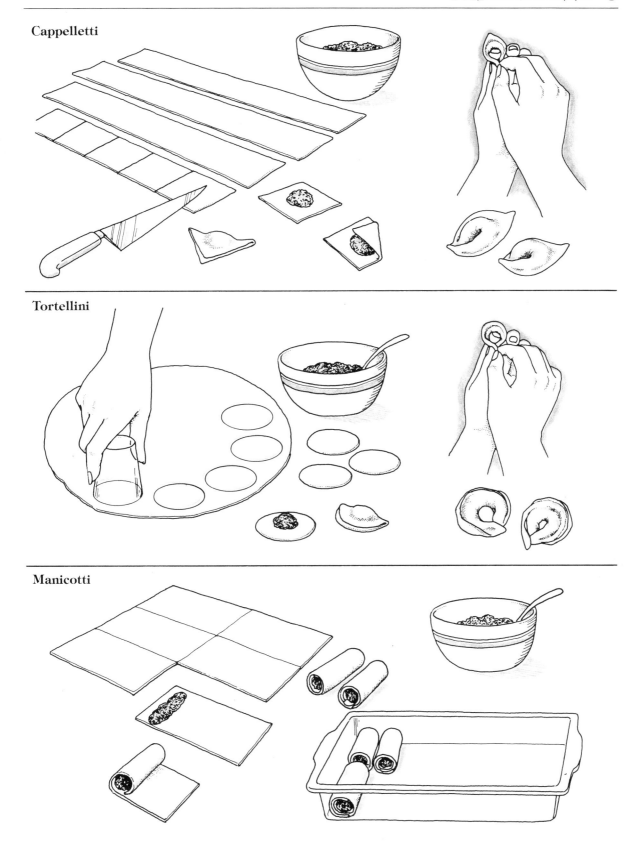

Ravioli

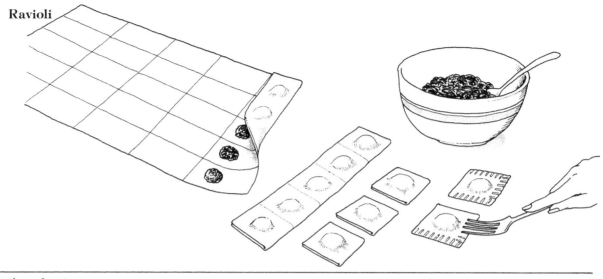

Agnolotti

Fettuccine and Other Noodles

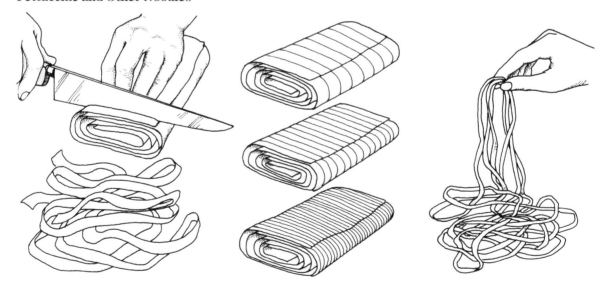

Ravioli

Divide the dough into 3 parts and roll out on a lightly floured board into sheets about 10 by 20 inches. Using a knife or pastry wheel, lightly mark the dough parallel to the 10-inch side at 4-inch intervals; mark it lengthwise at 2-inch intervals. Your dough will now be lightly marked into 4x2-inch strips.

Going across the bottom of the 10-inch side, place 1 teaspoon of filling (pages 12-13) about two-thirds of the way up on each strip. Fold the bottom half of the dough up to cover the first row of fillings. Cut across the dough to free the filled strip and cut into 5 individual ravioli. Seal the edges with a fork. Place on a lightly floured board. Repeat with the next row of 5 and continue until all the ravioli are filled.

Cook in a 6- to 8-quart pot of boiling salted water for about 6 to 7 minutes. Serve with your favorite sauce (pages 15-20).

Fried Ravioli

Prepare ravioli (above) with a filling of your choice.

Seal the edges well and allow the dough to dry for 30 minutes. Fill a deep skillet ¾ full of oil. Heat to 350° (a cube of bread starts sizzling at once). Fry the ravioli in batches until golden brown on one side. Turn and fry until browned on the other side. Serve with two bowls of dipping sauce: one tomato, the other bottled blue cheese dressing.

■ Great for hors d'oeuvres.

Agnolotti

Divide the dough into 3 parts and roll each into a 15-inch circle. Using a cookie cutter or glass, cut into 2½-inch circles.

Place a teaspoonful of filling (see pages 12-13) off center on each circle. Fold the pasta over to form a half-moon and seal the edges with a fork. Put on a lightly floured board.

Cook in a 6- to 8-quart pot of boiling salted water for about 6 to 7 minutes. Serve with your favorite sauce (pages 15-20).

Fettuccine and Other Noodles

Divide the dough into 2 or 3 parts and roll out into rectangles as thin as you can make them. You should be able to see through the dough.

Fold or roll the dough loosely from its short side down the length of the sheet. Using a sharp knife, cut the dough into ¼-inch strips (or narrower, if you wish). Shake the strips loose.

Cook in a 6- to 8-quart pot of boiling salted water until al dente. Drain and serve with your favorite sauce (pages 15-20).

> **Stuffed homemade pastas rise to the surface of the pot when they are almost done. Let them boil for another minute or two after they rise.**

Pasta Fillings

Ricotta Filling

2 cups ricotta cheese	1 teaspoon salt
2 eggs, beaten	¼ teaspoon pepper
½ cup grated Romano cheese	¼ teaspoon dried oregano leaves
3 tablespoons chopped parsley	¼ teaspoon garlic powder

Combine ingredients in a bowl and mix well.

Makes about 2½ cups.

Spinach and Ricotta Filling

1 cup ricotta cheese	1 teaspoon chopped parsley
1 package (10 ounces) frozen spinach, thawed, pureed in blender and drained	1 teaspoon salt
	¼ teaspoon pepper
2 eggs, beaten	¼ teaspoon dried oregano leaves
½ cup grated Romano cheese	½ teaspoon garlic powder

Combine ingredients in a bowl and mix well.

Makes about 2 cups.

Raisin and Ricotta Filling

2 cups ricotta cheese	1 cup grated Romano cheese
2 eggs, beaten	
1 cup raisins	1 teaspoon salt
¼ teaspoon nutmeg	¼ teaspoon pepper

Combine ingredients in a bowl and mix well.

Makes about 2 cups.

Chicken, Ricotta and Spinach Filling

1 cup minced cooked chicken	2 cloves garlic, minced
1 cup ricotta cheese	2 tablespoons chopped parsley
1 package (10 ounces) frozen spinach, thawed, pureed in blender and drained	¼ teaspoon pepper
	¼ teaspoon dried oregano leaves
2 eggs, beaten	
½ cup grated Romano cheese	¼ teaspoon nutmeg

Combine ingredients in a bowl and mix well.

Makes about 3 cups.

These fillings can be used to stuff your homemade pasta, commercial manicotti or jumbo shells. Mix and match with a Basic Sauce (pages 15-20) or any other sauce in this book that catches your fancy. Stuffed pastas are particularly good with Garlic Butter Sauce (page 20).

Chicken Filling

2 cups minced cooked
   chicken
2 eggs
2 tablespoons finely chopped
   parsley
½ cup grated Romano cheese
1 teaspoon salt
¼ teaspoon pepper
¼ teaspoon nutmeg

Combine ingredients in a bowl and mix well.

Makes about 2 cups.

Beef and Ricotta Filling

¾ pound ground beef
2 cups ricotta cheese
½ cup grated Romano
   cheese
3 eggs
1½ teaspoons salt
¼ teaspoon pepper
⅛ teaspoon dried oregano
   leaves
½ teaspoon garlic powder

Combine ingredients in a bowl and mix well.

Makes about 3 cups.

Beef, Ricotta and Spinach Filling

½ pound ground beef
1 cup ricotta cheese
1 package (10 ounces) frozen
   spinach, thawed, pureed
   in blender and drained
3 eggs, beaten
1 cup grated Romano cheese
   Pinch of nutmeg
1 teaspoon salt
¼ teaspoon pepper

Combine ingredients in a bowl and mix well.

Makes about 3 cups.

Veal Filling

1½ pounds ground veal
3 eggs, beaten
½ cup grated Romano cheese
1 tablespoon chopped
   parsley
¼ teaspoon nutmeg
1 teaspoon salt
¼ teaspoon pepper
¼ teaspoon garlic powder

Combine ingredients in a bowl and mix well.

Makes about 3 cups.

■ Different pastas use different amounts of fillings. Check your pasta yield (page 5) against the instructions for preparation to figure out how much filling you will need for a given pasta.

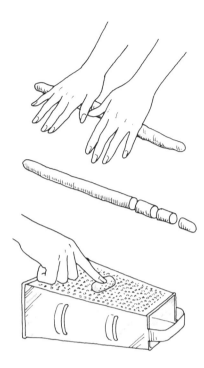

Potato Gnocchi

3 medium potatoes, boiled, peeled and mashed	2 eggs, beaten
1½ cups all-purpose flour	½ cup grated Romano cheese
2 tablespoons oil	½ teaspoon salt
	¼ teaspoon pepper

While still warm, place the mashed potatoes in a mixing bowl. Add the flour, oil, eggs, grated cheese, salt and pepper. Mix well until you can form the mixture into ropes. (Add more flour if needed.)

Taking a small amount at a time, roll the mixture into a rope ¾ inch thick. Cut into 1-inch lengths. Roll with your thumb on fine side of a lightly floured grater to form a little design. Place on a lightly floured board until ready to cook.

Cook in boiling salted water in a 6- to 8-quart pot until done (the dumplings will rise to the top of the water).

Serve with a sauce of your choice or with garlic butter.

6 to 8 servings.

■ Gnocchi are sticky. Use plenty of flour on the board and on your hands when shaping these dumplings.

Gnocchi are an Italian version of dumplings and are considered a pasta. They are delicious and well worth the trouble of making.

Green Gnocchi

3 potatoes, boiled, peeled and mashed	2 tablespoons oil
½ pound spinach, cooked, pureed in blender and drained	1½ cups all-purpose flour
	¼ teaspoon dried oregano leaves
2 eggs, beaten	½ teaspoon garlic powder
½ cup grated Romano cheese	1 teaspoon salt
	¼ teaspoon pepper

Combine the mashed potatoes, spinach, eggs, cheese, oil, flour and seasonings in a mixing bowl. Work well with your hand until the mixture can be formed into ropes. (You may have to add more flour).

Taking a small amount at a time, roll the mixture into a rope ¾ inch thick. Cut into 1½-inch lengths and place on a lightly floured board until ready to use.

Bring salted water to a boil in a 6- to 8-quart pot. Add the gnocchi in batches, removing with a slotted spoon as they rise to the surface.

Serve with a tomato sauce or melted butter and grated cheese.

4 to 6 servings.

Basic Sauces

Basic Tomato Sauce

½ cup oil
1 medium onion, finely chopped
2 cloves garlic, minced
1 can (28 ounces) plum tomatoes
1 can (6 ounces) tomato paste
1 can (6 ounces) water (use tomato paste can)

2 tablespoons chopped parsley
1 teaspoon dried basil leaves
1 teaspoon salt
¼ teaspoon pepper
¼ teaspoon dried oregano leaves

Heat the oil in a heavy 10- to 12-inch skillet over medium heat. Add the onion and garlic. Cook, stirring occasionally, until the onion is transparent. Add the tomatoes, crushing them in your hand as you add them, and the liquid from the can. Add remaining ingredients and stir to mix. Raise heat and bring the sauce to a boil.

Lower heat and simmer, uncovered, for 1½ to 2 hours. Stir occasionally to avoid burning.

Makes about 4 cups.

■ I belong to the old school and cook my sauces a long time, but not as long as my mother did. She cooked them all day. To my mind, a tomato sauce needs to be cooked for 2 hours or more to develop a mellow flavor and lose all the tartiness of the tomatoes. I can afford to do this because cooking is my business and the kitchen is my office. For those of you who can't spend the time, I point to my son. He makes delicious sauces that cook only 30 minutes. Taste your sauce after that period of time and if you like it, serve it! Rules are made to be broken, even my own. If the sauce still tastes tarty to you, however, try adding a pinch of baking soda or a teaspoon or so of sugar.

> Some people think crushing the tomatoes in a separate dish adds a gourmet touch. I think it just adds one more dirty dish, but if you don't like crushing the tomatoes with your hand this is another way of doing it.

Fresh Tomato Sauce

2 pounds very ripe plum tomatoes
½ cup oil
2 medium onions, finely chopped
3 cloves garlic, minced
1 teaspoon salt
¼ teaspoon pepper
¼ teaspoon dried oregano leaves
3 teaspoons dried basil leaves, crushed, or 6 to 8 fresh basil leaves
2 teaspoons chopped parsley

Plunge the tomatoes into boiling water for 12 seconds. Peel and chop coarsely. Heat the oil in a heavy 10- to 12-inch skillet over medium heat. Add the onions and garlic. Cook, stirring, until the onions are transparent. Add the tomatoes, salt, pepper, oregano, basil and parsley.

Cook, uncovered, over low heat for 2 hours. Stir occasionally to avoid burning.

Makes about 4 cups.

■ Any excess sauce can be frozen.

> **Too much oregano gives a dish a bitter taste. Use it sparingly, and if you prefer the powdered kind, use only half as much as the leaf.**

Mama D's Favorite Pasta Sauce

2 tablespoons oil
2 pounds pork spareribs, cut into serving pieces
1 medium onion, finely chopped
2 cloves garlic, minced
1 can (28 ounces) plum tomatoes
1 can (6 ounces) tomato paste
1 can (6 ounces) water (use tomato paste can)
1 teaspoon salt
½ teaspoon pepper
¼ teaspoon dried oregano leaves
½ teaspoon garlic powder
1½ teaspoons fennel seed

Heat the oil in a 5-quart flameproof casserole over medium-high heat and brown the spareribs. Add the onion and minced garlic and cook, stirring, until the onion is transparent. Add the tomatoes, crushing them in your hand as you add them, and the liquid from the can. Raise heat and add the remaining ingredients. Bring to a boil, stirring to mix.

Reduce heat and simmer, uncovered, for 2 hours or until the meat starts to fall away from the bone. Stir often to keep the sauce from sticking to the bottom of the pan.

4 to 6 servings.

■ This is a very good sauce, my favorite, and it can be served over any pasta. It can also be made ahead of time, set aside and frozen for a future occasion.

Marinara Sauce

3 tablespoons oil
2 small onions, finely
    chopped
2 cloves garlic, minced
2 large carrots, finely
    chopped
2 large stalks celery, finely
    chopped

1 can (28 ounces) plum
    tomatoes
1 teaspoon salt
¼ teaspoon pepper
¼ teaspoon dried oregano
    leaves

Heat the oil in a heavy 10- to 12-inch skillet over medium heat. Add the onions, garlic, carrots and celery and cook, stirring occasionally, until the onions are transparent. Add tomatoes, crushing them in your hand as you put them in, and the liquid from the can. Raise heat and add the remaining ingredients, stirring to blend. Bring to a boil.

Reduce heat and simmer, uncovered, for 1½ to 2 hours. Stir occasionally to avoid burning.

Makes about 4 cups.

■ This sauce is good with any pasta and is the base for many seafood sauces. Try also serving or cooking fish with it.

Fresh Mushroom Sauce

3 tablespoons oil
1 pound mushrooms, sliced
2 medium onions, finely
    chopped
3 cloves garlic, minced
1 can (28 ounces) plum
    tomatoes
1 teaspoon salt
¼ teaspoon pepper
¼ teaspoon dried oregano
    leaves

1 tablespoon chopped parsley
3 or 4 fresh basil leaves or
    ¼ teaspoon dried basil
    leaves
1 can (6 ounces) tomato
    paste
1 can (6 ounces) water
    (use tomato paste can)

Heat the oil in a heavy 10- to 12-inch skillet over medium heat. Add the mushrooms, onions and garlic. Cook, stirring occasionally, until the onions are transparent. Add the tomatoes, crushing them in your hand as you add them, and the liquid from the can. Raise heat and add remaining ingredients. Stir to blend and bring to a boil.

Lower heat and simmer, uncovered, for 1½ to 2 hours. Stir occasionally to avoid burning.

Makes about 4 cups.

Ham and Tomato Sauce

3 tablespoons oil	1 teaspoon salt
½ pound prosciutto, chopped	¼ teaspoon pepper
2 small onions, finely chopped	¼ teaspoon dried oregano leaves
2 cloves garlic, minced	1 tablespoon dried basil leaves
1 can (28 ounces) plum tomatoes	

Heat the oil in a heavy 10- to 12-inch skillet over medium heat. Add the prosciutto, onions and garlic. Cook, stirring occasionally, until the onions are transparent. Add the tomatoes, crushing them in your hand as you add them, and the liquid from the can. Raise the heat, add the remaining ingredients and stir well to blend. Bring to a boil.

Lower heat and simmer, uncovered, for about 2 hours. Stir from time to time to prevent burning.

Makes about 3 cups.

Bolognese Sauce

1 pound boneless beef chuck or round	1 can (4 ounces) mushroom stems and pieces, drained
½ pound boneless veal shoulder	1 cup dry white wine
½ pound boneless fresh pork butt	2 tablespoons chopped parsley
2 tablespoons butter	2 teaspoons dried basil leaves, crushed
2 tablespoons oil	¼ teaspoon nutmeg
2 small onions, chopped	1 teaspoon salt
2 cloves garlic, minced	¼ teaspoon pepper
2 stalks celery, chopped	¼ teaspoon dried oregano leaves
2 cans (28 ounces each) plum tomatoes	

Cut the beef, veal and pork into ¾-inch cubes. Melt the butter with the oil in a 4-quart flameproof casserole over medium-high heat. Add the meat and sauté, turning to brown evenly.

Reduce heat to medium and add the onions, garlic and celery. Cook, stirring occasionally, until the onions are transparent. Add the tomatoes, crushing them in your hand as you add them, and the liquid from the can. Add the remaining ingredients and stir to mix. Raise heat and bring to a boil. Lower heat and simmer, uncovered, for 2½ hours. Stir occasionally to avoid burning.

Makes about 8 cups.

Tomato and Mushroom Meat Sauce

2 tablespoons oil
2 green peppers, seeded and
    coarsely chopped
2 medium onions, coarsely
    chopped
1 clove garlic, minced
1 pound ground beef
1 can (4 ounces) sliced
    mushrooms, drained

1 can (29 ounces) tomato
    puree
3 sprigs parsley
8 fresh basil leaves or
    ½ teaspoon dried basil
    leaves
1 teaspoon salt
¼ teaspoon pepper

Heat the oil in a heavy 10- to 12-inch skillet over medium heat. Add the green peppers, onions and garlic. Cook, stirring occasionally, until the onions are transparent. Add the ground beef, breaking up the chunks with a wooden fork, and cook until browned. Add the mushrooms, tomato puree, parsley, basil, salt and pepper. Bring to a boil.

Lower heat and simmer, uncovered, for about 1½ to 2 hours. Stir from time to time to prevent burning.

Makes about 5 cups.

I always use Italian parsley: fresh when I can get it and freeze-dried when I can't. I like its pungent taste, although its flat leaf makes it inferior to the curly variety as a garnish. You use whichever you like better.

Cacciatora Sauce

4 tablespoons oil
2 small onions, finely
    chopped
3 cloves garlic, minced
2 green peppers, seeded and
    cut into slivers
1 can (28 ounces) plum
    tomatoes

1 can (8 ounces) sliced
    mushrooms, drained
¼ cup Chablis or sauterne
1 tablespoon chopped parsley
1 teaspoon salt
¼ teaspoon pepper
¼ teaspoon dried oregano
    leaves

Heat the oil in a heavy 10- to 12-inch skillet over medium heat. Add the onions, garlic and green peppers and cook, stirring from time to time, until the onions are transparent. Raise heat and add the tomatoes, crushing them in your hand as you add them, and the liquid from the can. Add the remaining ingredients and stir well to blend. Bring to a boil.

Reduce heat and simmer, uncovered, for about 2 hours. Stir occasionally to avoid burning.

Makes about 4 cups.

■ Besides being good over any pasta, this sauce is delicious cooked with or served over baked chicken. At home I used to make it with concentrated tomato soup added to the tomatoes and a sweet Concord wine instead of white wine. My boys loved it.

Pesto Sauce

3 cups fresh basil leaves	½ cup pine nuts
½ cup oil	1 teaspoon salt
¾ cup grated Romano cheese	½ teaspoon pepper

Place the ingredients in a blender and puree to a smooth paste. If the pesto seems too dry, stir in a few tablespoons of melted butter. Scrape the sauce into a serving bowl.

To serve, put the pasta on warmed plates and let people help themselves to the sauce.

Makes about 2 cups.

■ Pesto is usually served with fettuccine, but it is also delicious with any pasta. It keeps well in the refrigerator.

Mama D's Pesto Sauce

1 large bunch parsley with stems, chopped	½ cup grated Romano cheese
1 cup fresh basil leaves	1 teaspoon salt
2 tablespoons butter, melted	¼ teaspoon pepper
½ cup oil	¼ teaspoon dried oregano leaves
4 cloves garlic	½ cup pine nuts

I use parsley stems as well as parsley leaves because it's so much more economical. But to avoid clogging the blender, you have to chop the stems before putting them in.

Place the ingredients in a blender and puree to a smooth paste. Scrape the sauce into a serving bowl.

Serve and store in the same manner as the preceding Pesto Sauce.

Makes about 3 cups.

Garlic Butter Sauce

1 cup butter	¼ teaspoon pepper
4 cloves garlic, minced	¼ teaspoon dried oregano leaves
1 teaspoon salt	

Melt the butter in a heavy 8-inch skillet over medium heat. Add the garlic, salt, pepper and oregano. Cook, stirring, until the garlic is lightly browned. Toss with pasta and serve with grated cheese.

4 to 6 servings.

Bowties with Eggplant Meatballs

4 cups tomato sauce	1 pound bowties
Eggplant Meatballs (below)	½ cup grated Romano cheese

Prepare the tomato sauce and meatballs. When the sauce is almost done, add the meatballs to the sauce. Cook the pasta according to package directions until al dente. Drain and put onto a warmed platter. Stir in about 2 cups of the sauce and top with the meatballs. Sprinkle with the Romano and serve hot with the remaining sauce on the side.

4 to 6 servings.

Eggplant Meatballs

1 medium eggplant (about 1½ pounds), peeled and diced	¼ cup chopped parsley
	¼ teaspoon fennel seed
	¼ teaspoon pepper
1 pound ground beef	1 teaspoon salt
3 slices stale bread	¼ teaspoon dried oregano leaves
3 eggs	
½ cup grated Romano cheese	¼ teaspoon garlic powder

Cook the eggplant in boiling water until soft. Put into a large bowl with the beef. Soak the bread in water and squeeze dry. Tear the bread into pieces and add to the bowl with the remaining ingredients. Mix lightly, but thoroughly, with your hands.

Grease your hands lightly and roll the mixture into balls, each about the size of a golf ball. Place in a greased, shallow baking pan and bake in a preheated 375° oven for 30 to 35 minutes or until browned and cooked through.

Makes about 16 balls.

> While you wouldn't want to substitute lasagne for soup noodles in recipes, many pastas are interchangeable. God gave you sense! Use it—and the pasta of your choice in any recipe.

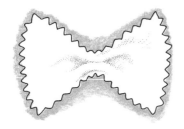

Bowties are sometimes called butterflies. Use any noodle in their place or, if you enjoy amusing shapes, use cavatelli, rotelle or riccini.

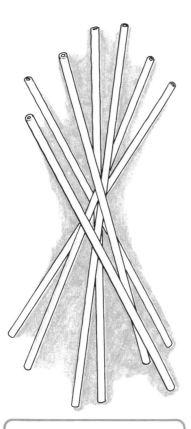

Bucatini is called spaghetti with a hole, but it is really the thinnest of the macaroni family. Use spaghetti or perciatelli if you can't find bucatini.

Bowties with Pomidoro Pelati

1 tablespoon butter	2 tablespoons chopped parsley
2 tablespoons oil	
2 small onions, finely chopped	1 tablespoon dried basil leaves
¼ pound prosciutto, shredded	1 teaspoon salt
	¼ teaspoon pepper
1 cup chicken broth	1 pound bowties
1 can (28 ounces) plum tomatoes, drained	1 cup grated Parmesan or Romano cheese

Melt the butter in the oil in a heavy 10- to 12-inch skillet over medium heat. Add the onions. Cook, stirring enough to prevent burning, until the onions are transparent. Add the prosciutto and simmer for 2 or 3 minutes. Add the broth. Break up the tomatoes with your hand and add them, one at a time, to the skillet. Stir in the parsley, basil, salt and pepper. Bring the mixture to a boil, then reduce heat and simmer, uncovered, for 30 to 45 minutes.

Cook the pasta according to package directions until al dente. Drain and place on a warmed platter. Stir in 2 cups of the sauce and about ½ cup grated cheese. Serve with the remaining sauce and cheese on the side.

4 to 6 servings.

Bucatini with Anchovy, Garlic and Oil Sauce

2 tablespoons butter	¼ teaspoon pepper
½ cup olive oil	¼ teaspoon dried oregano leaves
5 cloves garlic, minced	
1 can (2 ounces) anchovy fillets	1 pound bucatini
	½ cup grated Romano cheese

Melt the butter in the oil in a heavy 8-inch skillet. Add the garlic and cook, stirring, until golden. Make sure the garlic doesn't burn. Add the anchovies, with the oil from the can, to the skillet. Sprinkle with the pepper and oregano. Reduce heat and cook slowly, uncovered, for about 30 minutes.

Cook the pasta according to package directions until al dente. Drain and place on a warmed platter. Pour the sauce over the pasta and stir gently. Sprinkle with the cheese and serve.

4 to 6 servings.

■ If you like the flavor of garlic but don't enjoy eating it, crush the cloves of garlic instead of mincing them. Cook them in the oil until they are golden. Discard them and continue with the recipe.

Cavatelli with Lima Bean Sauce

1 tablespoon butter
1 tablespoon oil
½ pound bacon, cut into pieces
2 small onions, finely chopped

2 cloves garlic, minced
1 can (16 ounces) lima beans
1 pound cavatelli
½ cup grated Parmesan cheese

Melt the butter in the oil in a heavy 8-inch skillet over medium heat. Add the bacon and cook, stirring as needed, until the bacon is crisp. Remove the bacon from the skillet with a slotted spoon and reserve. Add the onions and garlic to the skillet and cook until the onions are transparent. Add the bacon and lima beans, liquid and all, and simmer, uncovered, for 10 minutes.

Cook the pasta according to package directions until al dente. Drain and put into a warmed deep bowl. Stir in the lima bean mixture. Add the cheese and mix well. Serve hot.

4 to 6 servings.

> **Cavatelli are short and curly noodles that look a little like the medium shells (maruzzelle) that can be used in their place. Riccini and rotelle also make good substitutes.**

Papa V's Ditalini and Red Kidney Beans

1 pound ditalini
3 tablespoons olive oil
1 large clove garlic, minced
  Dash of crushed red pepper
⅛ teaspoon dried oregano leaves

⅛ teaspoon dried basil leaves
1 can (20 ounces) red kidney beans
  Grated Parmesan or Romano cheese

Put the pasta on to cook, following package directions.

While the pasta is cooking, heat the oil in a heavy 8-inch skillet over medium heat. Add the garlic, red pepper, oregano and basil. Cook, stirring, until the garlic is golden but not burned. Add the beans, liquid and all, to the skillet and heat almost to a boil. Taste for seasoning and add salt if necessary.

When the pasta is al dente, drain and put it into a warmed deep bowl. Add the beans and mix thoroughly. If too dry for your taste, add a tablespoon or two of olive oil. Serve with grated cheese on the side.

4 to 6 servings.

■ This recipe was given to me by Vincent Picarello. I tried it with canned fava beans, too, and it's good either way.

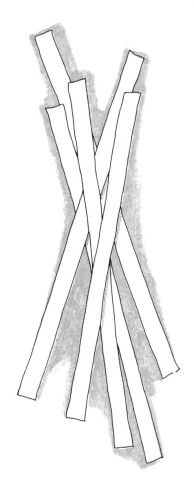

Fettuccelle with Red Lobster Sauce

6 frozen lobster tails, boiled
   according to package
   directions
2 tablespoons butter
3 tablespoons oil
2 medium onions, chopped
2 cloves garlic, minced
1 stalk celery, chopped

1 can (29 ounces) tomato
   puree
1 teaspoon salt
½ teaspoon pepper
¼ teaspoon dried oregano
   leaves
1 pound fettuccelle

Shell the lobster meat, reserving the shells, and cut the meat into small pieces. Melt the butter in the oil in a heavy 10- to 12-inch skillet over medium heat. Add the onions, garlic and celery and cook, stirring, until the onions are transparent. Add the tomato puree, salt, pepper, oregano and the lobster shells.

Bring the mixture to a boil. Lower the heat and simmer, uncovered, for 1 hour or more until the sauce is thickened. Stir occasionally to avoid burning. Remove the lobster shells and add the lobster meat. Simmer for 5 minutes or until heated through.

When the sauce is almost done, cook the pasta according to package directions until al dente. Drain and place on a warmed platter. Pour about 2 cups of the sauce over the pasta and mix well. Serve the remaining sauce on the side.

4 to 6 servings.

Fettuccelle is a flattened macaroni. Good substitutes are any of the noodles, such as fettuccine, margherite or mafalde.

Mama D's Fettuccine Alfredo

1 pound fettuccine
8 tablespoons butter
1 can (4 ounces) sliced
   mushrooms, drained
½ teaspoon salt
¼ teaspoon pepper

¼ teaspoon dried oregano
   leaves
½ teaspoon garlic powder
¼ cup grated Romano cheese
¼ cup shredded mozzarella
   cheese

Put the fettuccine on to cook, following package directions. While the pasta is cooking, melt the butter in a skillet. Add the mushrooms, salt, pepper, oregano and garlic powder and heat the mushrooms through.

When the fettuccine is just al dente, drain and place it in a shallow baking dish. Toss with the Romano cheese and then stir in the butter mixture. Sprinkle with the mozzarella cheese and place in a preheated 375° oven for about 5 minutes or until the cheese is melted but not browned. Serve hot.

4 to 6 servings.

Fettuccine with Creamed Spinach

2 tablespoons butter	1 teaspoon salt
1½ pounds spinach, washed, cooked and shredded	¼ teaspoon pepper
	¼ teaspoon garlic powder
3 tablespoons butter	1 small onion, minced
6 slices bacon, cut into small pieces	1 pound fettuccine
	⅔ cup grated Romano cheese
4 tablespoons flour	
1¼ cups milk, heated	

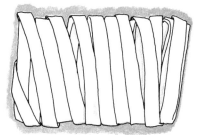

Melt the 2 tablespoons butter in a heavy 10- to 12-inch skillet and add the spinach. Cook, stirring, until blended. Set aside.

Melt the 3 tablespoons butter in a saucepan. Cook the bacon in the butter until it is almost crisp. Remove with a slotted spoon and reserve. Blend the flour into the bacon drippings and butter. Gradually add the milk, stirring to prevent lumps. Simmer, stirring occasionally, until the sauce is smooth and thickened. Add the salt, pepper, garlic powder and onion. Combine the sauce and the spinach and simmer an additional 5 minutes.

While the sauce is simmering, cook the pasta according to package directions until just al dente. Drain the pasta and place in a shallow baking dish. Sprinkle with the cheese. Pour the sauce over the pasta and sprinkle the bacon over the top. Place in a preheated 375° oven for 5 minutes or until ingredients are hot and bubbling.

4 to 6 servings.

> **Fettuccine is a very popular noodle. Fans say that sauces stick better to it than to other pastas, but you can always use what you like best. Green fettuccine is made with spinach.**

Paglia e Fieno (Straw and Hay)

3 tablespoons butter	¼ cup grated Romano cheese
3 tablespoons oil	1 teaspoon salt
2 cloves garlic, minced	¼ teaspoon pepper
½ pound green noodles	⅛ teaspoon dried oregano leaves
½ pound wide fettuccine	
1 cup ricotta cheese, at room temperature	

Melt the butter in the oil in a heavy skillet over medium heat. Add the garlic and cook, stirring, until the garlic is golden. Set aside.

Cook the pastas in two separate pots according to package directions until al dente. Combine in a warmed deep bowl. Add the butter and oil mixture, the cheeses and the seasonings. Stir gently together and serve hot.

4 to 6 servings.

Rolled Lasagne

2 cups ricotta cheese
2 eggs, beaten
½ cup grated Romano cheese
1 teaspoon salt
¼ teaspoon pepper
¼ teaspoon dried oregano
   leaves
¼ teaspoon garlic powder
¼ teaspoon nutmeg
½ pound lasagne, cooked and
   put into cold water
4 cups tomato sauce

Combine all of the ingredients except the lasagne and sauce; mix well. Spread cheese filling on a strip of lasagne and roll up. Place in a baking dish. Continue this process until all the lasagne is used up. Pour the sauce over the noodles. Cover firmly with aluminum foil and bake in a preheated 375° oven for 45 minutes.

4 to 6 servings.

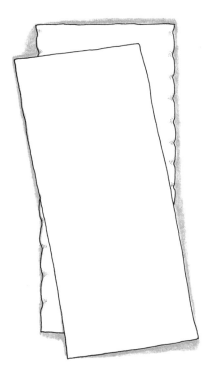

Lasagne are the widest of the noodles and are served baked in layers with filling in between. You've never tasted a good lasagne until you've made it from scratch with your own dough (pages 5 - 7).

Baked Eggplant Lasagne

1 large eggplant (about
   2½ pounds)
1 teaspoon salt
¼ teaspoon pepper
¼ teaspoon dried oregano
   leaves
¼ teaspoon garlic powder
1 cup all-purpose flour
2 eggs
2 tablespoons water
   Oil for frying
2½ cups tomato sauce
½ pound lasagne, cooked
   and put into cold water
1 cup grated Romano cheese
2 cups ricotta cheese
2 cups shredded mozzarella
   cheese

Peel the eggplant and cut lengthwise into slices ¼ inch thick. Mix the salt, pepper, oregano and garlic powder with the flour. Beat the eggs with the water. Flour the eggplant slices and dip in the egg mixture. Add enough oil to a heavy 10- to 12-inch skillet to cover the bottom of the pan. Heat over medium-high heat. Fry the eggplant slices in batches until golden brown on one side; turn and fry until golden brown on second side. Drain on paper towels.

Pour ¼ inch hot water into the bottom of a 13½x9½x2-inch baking dish. Add ½ cup of the tomato sauce. Place a layer of lasagne in the sauce and cover with a layer of eggplant slices. Sprinkle with about 4 tablespoons of the Romano cheese. Dab with 1 cup of the ricotta and sprinkle with ⅔ cup of the mozzarella. Repeat, ending with a final layer of lasagne. Pour enough of the sauce over the top to cover generously. Sprinkle with the remaining Romano and mozzarella. Cover tightly with aluminum foil. Bake in a preheated 375° oven for 45 minutes.

4 to 6 servings.

Lasagne with Shrimp

2 cups ricotta cheese	3 tablespoons butter, melted
2 teaspoons chopped parsley	2½ cups tomato sauce
2 eggs, beaten	½ pound lasagne, cooked and put into cold water
½ cup grated Romano cheese	1 pound shrimp, shelled, deveined and cooked
1 teaspoon salt	½ cup grated Romano cheese
¼ teaspoon pepper	1 cup shredded mozzarella cheese
¼ teaspoon dried oregano leaves	
¼ teaspoon garlic powder	

Put the ricotta into a mixing bowl. Add the parsley, eggs, ½ cup Romano cheese, salt, pepper, oregano and garlic powder.

Spread the melted butter over the bottom of a 13½x9x2-inch baking dish. Pour ½ cup sauce over the butter. Cover with a layer of lasagne. Put half the ricotta mixture over the lasagne, then half the shrimp. Cover with another layer of lasagne, the remaining ricotta and shrimp and end with a layer of lasagne on top. Cover generously with the sauce. Sprinkle with ½ cup Romano and then mozzarella. Cover firmly with aluminum foil. Bake in a preheated 375° oven for 45 minutes.

4 to 6 servings.

> **Stuffed, layered lasagne is served cut into squares like pieces of cake. I like to top each portion with additional sauce and cheese.**

Meatless Lasagne

2½ cups tomato sauce	⅛ teaspoon dried oregano leaves
½ pound lasagne, cooked and put into cold water	¼ teaspoon garlic powder
2 cups ricotta cheese	1 teaspoon chopped parsley
2 eggs, beaten	¾ cup grated Romano cheese
1 teaspoon salt	1 cup shredded mozzarella cheese
¼ teaspoon pepper	

Add ¼ inch hot water to a 13½x9x2-inch baking dish. Pour in ½ cup of the tomato sauce and cover the bottom of the pan with lasagne. Combine the ricotta with the eggs, seasonings and ½ cup of the Romano cheese in a bowl and mix well.

Spread half the filling on the lasagne. Repeat with another layer of lasagne and the remaining filling. Cover with a final layer of lasagne. Spoon enough of the sauce over all to cover generously. Sprinkle with the remaining ¼ cup Romano cheese and then with the mozzarella. Cover firmly with aluminum foil and bake in a preheated 375° oven for 45 minutes.

4 to 6 servings.

Linguine with Asparagus

1 pound asparagus	¼ teaspoon dried oregano leaves
1 pound linguine	
1 teaspoon salt	3 tablespoons olive oil
¼ teaspoon pepper	Grated Romano cheese

Clean the asparagus and snap off the tough ends. Cut the remaining spears into 1-inch pieces.

Put the pasta on to cook, following package directions. Cook the asparagus in boiling salted water for about 4 minutes or until tender but still crisp, then drain.

When the pasta is al dente, drain and put into a warmed deep bowl with the asparagus. Sprinkle with the salt, pepper and oregano. Add the olive oil and mix well. Toss with 2 or 3 tablespoons of grated cheese and serve hot with additional cheese on the side.

4 to 6 servings.

■ Instead of fresh asparagus, you may use 1 package (10 ounces) frozen asparagus tips cooked according to package directions.

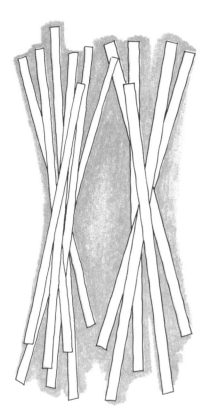

Linguine and linguine fini are flat spaghetti and flat spaghettini. The former is wider and traditional with a clam sauce, but if you like spaghetti better, use it. Green linguine is made with spinach.

Linguine with John's White Clam Sauce

4 tablespoons oil	⅛ teaspoon dried oregano leaves
4 cloves garlic, minced	
2 tablespoons chopped parsley	12 little neck clams, well scrubbed
1 tablespoon chopped fresh basil leaves or 1 teaspoon dried basil leaves	2 cans (8 ounces each) minced clams
¼ teaspoon pepper	1 pound linguine

Heat the oil in a heavy skillet that will hold the clams in one layer. Add the garlic, parsley, basil, pepper, oregano and little neck clams. Cook over medium-high heat, shaking the pan occasionally, until the clams open. Remove the clams from the pan and add the 2 cans of clams, liquid and all, to the skillet. Bring to a boil and cook, stirring, for 5 minutes.

While the sauce is cooking, boil the pasta according to package directions until al dente. Drain and put onto a warmed platter. Pour the clam sauce over the pasta and top with the clams in shells.

Serves 4 to 6.

■ This recipe and the one that follows are my son John's. They're mighty good.

Linguine with John's Red Clam Sauce

4 tablespoons oil	1 can (28 ounces) plum
4 cloves garlic, minced	tomatoes, drained and
2 tablespoons chopped	crushed
parsley	12 little neck clams, well
1 tablespoon chopped fresh	scrubbed
basil leaves or 1 teaspoon	2 cans (8 ounces each)
dried basil leaves	minced clams
¼ teaspoon pepper	1 pound linguine
⅛ teaspoon dried oregano	
leaves	

Heat the oil in a heavy skillet that will hold the clams in one layer. Add the garlic, parsley, basil, pepper, oregano, crushed tomatoes and the little neck clams. Cook over high heat until the clams open. Remove the clams from the pan and add the 2 cans of clams, liquid and all. Bring to a boil. Lower heat and simmer, uncovered, for 30 minutes. Add the clams in shells just before serving to heat through.

While the sauce is simmering, cook the pasta according to package directions until al dente. Drain and put onto a warmed platter. Spoon the sauce over the pasta and top with the clams in shells.

4 to 6 servings.

> **A pasta cooked in too small an amount of water sticks together and is gummy. You need 4 quarts of water and 1 tablespoon of salt for 1 pound of pasta. Get the water really boiling before you throw the pasta in. Stir to separate the strands.**

Linguine with Peas

2 tablespoons butter	1 teaspoon salt
2 tablespoons oil	½ teaspoon pepper
2 small onions, finely	¼ teaspoon dried oregano
chopped	leaves
2 cloves garlic, minced	1 can (17 ounces) peas
2 medium stalks celery with	1 pound linguine
leaves, finely chopped	½ cup grated Romano cheese
1 tablespoon chopped parsley	

Melt the butter in the oil in a heavy 8-inch skillet over medium heat. Add the onions, garlic and celery and cook, stirring occasionally, until the onions are transparent. Add the parsley, salt, pepper, oregano and the peas, liquid and all. Bring to a boil. Lower heat and simmer, uncovered, for 15 minutes.

While the peas are simmering, cook the pasta according to package directions until al dente. Drain and put into a warmed deep bowl. Add the pea mixture and sprinkle with cheese. Toss gently and serve immediately.

4 to 6 servings.

Green Linguine with Liver Balls

1 recipe Basic Tomato Sauce (page 15)	1 pound green linguine
Liver Balls (below)	½ cup grated Parmesan cheese

Prepare the tomato sauce and liver balls. When the sauce is about ready to serve, add the liver balls to heat through. Cook the pasta according to package directions until al dente. Drain and put onto a warmed platter.

Mix the pasta with about half of the sauce and top with the liver balls. Sprinkle with cheese and serve hot with the remaining sauce on the side.

4 to 6 servings.

■ This dish makes a delicious and nutritious low-cost dinner.

Liver Balls

1 pound beef liver	2 tablespoons finely chopped onion
2 ounces pork fat	
4 slices stale bread	1 teaspoon salt
3 eggs	¼ teaspoon pepper
¼ cup grated Parmesan cheese	Flour
	Oil or butter for frying

Chop the liver and pork fat almost to a pulp. Place in a large bowl. Soak the bread in water and squeeze dry. Tear bread into pieces and add to the bowl together with the eggs, Parmesan, onion, salt and pepper. Mix well with your hands. Form the mixture into balls the size of walnuts. Flour the balls and fry in a small amount of oil until brown and cooked through.

Makes about 30 walnut-size balls.

> I like Romano cheese better than Parmesan because it's more pungent. But I'm no authority when it comes to someone else's mouth.

Linguine with Béchamel Sauce

3 tablespoons butter	½ teaspoon salt
3 tablespoons flour	1 pound linguine
2 cups hot milk	½ cup grated Romano cheese

Melt the butter in a saucepan. Add the flour and cook, stirring, over low heat for 2 minutes. Add the milk gradually, bit by bit, stirring until the mixture is smooth. Simmer until the sauce thickens. Add salt. Cook the pasta until al dente. Drain and toss with the sauce. Put into a baking dish. Sprinkle with the cheese and bake in a preheated 375° oven for about 10 minutes.

4 to 6 servings.

Linguine with Eggplant Sauce

2 tablespoons butter
2 tablespoons oil
2 medium onions, finely chopped
2 cloves garlic, minced
1 medium eggplant (about 1½ pounds), peeled and cut into cubes
1 can (28 ounces) plum tomatoes
3 small carrots, finely chopped
1 teaspoon salt
¼ teaspoon dried basil leaves
¼ cup pine nuts
1 pound linguine
½ cup grated Parmesan cheese

Melt the butter in the oil in a heavy 10- to 12-inch skillet over medium heat. Add the onions, garlic and eggplant. Cook, stirring occasionally, until the onions are transparent. Add the tomatoes, crushing them in your hand, and the liquid from the can. Stir in the carrots, salt and basil. Bring to a boil, lower heat and simmer, uncovered, for about 1½ hours. Stir from time to time to avoid burning. Just before serving, mix in the pine nuts.

When the sauce is almost ready, cook the pasta according to package directions until al dente. Drain and put into a warmed deep bowl. Add the sauce and mix gently. Sprinkle with the cheese and serve.

4 to 6 servings.

Plum tomatoes, fresh or canned, are the best variety for cooking. When buying them canned, however, get the American ones. They're just as good and a lot cheaper than the imported Italian tomatoes.

Linguine Fini with Walnut Sauce

1 pound linguine fini
2 cups walnuts
1 cup pine nuts
2 cloves garlic
2 tablespoons chopped parsley
2 tablespoons butter, melted
2 tablespoons oil
1 cup ricotta cheese
2 tablespoons water
1 teaspoon salt
¼ teaspoon pepper
¼ teaspoon dried oregano leaves
½ cup grated Romano cheese

Put the pasta on to cook, following package directions. While it is boiling, combine the remaining ingredients except the Romano in a blender. (You will probably have to do this in batches.) Blend until creamy.

When the pasta is al dente, drain and place in a warmed deep bowl. Toss with the sauce and sprinkle with Romano cheese.

4 to 6 servings.

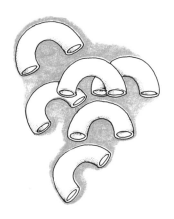

Elbow macaroni is a bent tube. Ditali, another short tube, is a good substitute as are maruzzine and maruzzelle (small and medium shells).

Macaroni and Chicken Pie

3 tablespoons butter	1 teaspoon salt
4 tablespoons oil	¼ teaspoon pepper
2 slices prosciutto, finely chopped	¼ teaspoon dried oregano leaves
2 medium carrots, coarsely grated	½ teaspoon garlic powder
2 small onions, finely chopped	1½ cups chicken broth
1 small stalk celery, finely chopped	½ pound elbow macaroni, cooked and rinsed in cold water
2½ cups cubed cooked chicken	¼ cup grated Parmesan cheese
1 can (4 ounces) sliced mushrooms, drained	Pie Crust (below)

Melt the butter in the oil in a 3-quart pot. Add the prosciutto, carrots, onions and celery. Cook, stirring occasionally, until the onions are transparent. Add the chicken and mushrooms. Stir well and season with the salt, pepper, oregano and garlic powder. Add the broth. Bring to a boil, lower heat and simmer, uncovered, for 30 minutes. Add the pasta and cheese, stirring them in.

Prepare the pie crust. Roll one pastry circle around the rolling pin and unroll into a 9-inch pie pan. Cut the dough evenly ½ inch from the edge of the pan. Pour the filling into the pie pan and cover with the top crust. Fold the edges under and flute. Cut slits here and there and brush with the egg mixture.

Bake in a preheated 375° oven for 30 to 35 minutes or until the crust is golden and the filling bubbling.

6 servings.

Pie Crust

2¼ cups all-purpose flour	4 tablespoons cold water
1 teaspoon salt	1 egg beaten with
⅔ cup lard	1 tablespoon water
¼ teaspoon vinegar	

Combine the flour and salt in a mixing bowl. Cut in the lard until the dough is like coarse meal. Mix in the vinegar and then the water, 1 tablespoon at a time, until the dough almost cleans the side of the bowl. Form into two balls. Roll each out on a lightly floured board until it is 2 inches larger than an inverted 9-inch pie pan.

Makes one 2-crust 9-inch pie or two 9-inch shells.

Macaroni and Sausage Pie

½ pound sweet Italian sausages	½ cup grated Romano cheese
1 recipe Pie Crust (page 32)	1 teaspoon salt
1½ cups elbow macaroni, cooked and rinsed in cold water	¼ teaspoon pepper
	¼ teaspoon dried oregano leaves
	¼ teaspoon garlic powder
8 eggs, beaten	1 teaspoon chopped parsley

Put the sausages into a shallow baking pan and bake in a preheated 375° oven for 40 minutes, turning them halfway through the cooking. Cut into ¼-inch pieces.

Prepare the pastry. Roll one of the pastry circles around the rolling pin and unroll into a 9-inch pie pan. Cut the dough evenly ½ inch from the edge of the pan.

Combine the sausages and remaining ingredients. Pour into the pie pan and cover with the top crust. Fold the edges under and flute. Cut slits here and there and brush with the egg mixture. Bake in a preheated 350° oven for 1 hour. Serve hot.

6 servings.

> **Pasta that is to be baked after cooking should be a little underdone or just al dente when you take it from the pot. Rinsing it in cold water keeps it from sticking and stops the cooking. It will cook more while it's baking.**

Macaroni with Sausage Sauce

4 tablespoons oil	1 teaspoon salt
1 pound sweet Italian sausage, cut into pieces	¼ teaspoon pepper
2 onions, finely chopped	¼ teaspoon dried oregano leaves
3 cloves garlic, minced	1 pound elbow macaroni
1 can (16 ounces) plum tomatoes	½ cup grated Romano cheese

Heat the oil in a heavy 8-inch skillet over medium-high heat. Add the sausage and cook, turning, until lightly browned on all sides. Lower the heat to medium and add the onions and garlic. Cook until the onions are transparent.

Drain the pan of half the fat and add the tomatoes, crushing them in your hand as you add them, along with the liquid from the can. Add the seasonings, bring to a boil and lower the heat. Simmer, uncovered, for about 1 hour. Stir occasionally to avoid burning.

Cook the pasta according to package directions until al dente. Drain and put into a warmed deep bowl. Mix the sauce into the pasta. Sprinkle with cheese and serve.

4 to 6 servings.

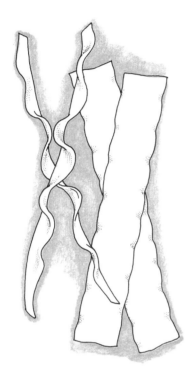

Mafalde is a broad noodle with curly edges, and margherite is a narrower, wavy noodle. Fettuccine or any other noodles can be used in their place.

Mafalde with Tuna Sauce

4 tablespoons oil	1 can (2 ounces) anchovy fillets, drained
2 cloves garlic, minced	1 tablespoon capers, chopped
1 can (28 ounces) plum tomatoes	1 can (7 ounces) tuna, drained and flaked
½ teaspoon salt	1 pound mafalde
¼ teaspoon pepper	
⅛ teaspoon dried oregano leaves	

Heat the oil in a heavy 10- to 12-inch skillet over medium heat. Add the garlic and cook, stirring, until the garlic is golden. Add the tomatoes, crushing them in your hand as you add them, and the liquid from the can. Add the remaining ingredients except the pasta. Bring to a boil, lower heat and simmer, uncovered, for about 2½ hours or until the sauce is a little on the thick side. Stir occasionally to prevent burning.

When the sauce is almost ready, cook the pasta according to package directions until al dente. Drain and put into a warmed deep bowl. Add half the sauce and mix gently. Serve with the remaining sauce on the side.

4 to 6 servings.

Margherite with Ham and Eggs

1 pound margherite	½ cup grated Parmesan cheese
2 tablespoons butter	Salt to taste
2 tablespoons oil	½ teaspoon pepper
½ pound prosciutto, cut into slivers	3 eggs, well beaten

Put the pasta on to cook, following package directions.

Melt the butter in the oil in a heavy skillet over medium heat. Add the prosciutto and cook, stirring, until the ham is lightly browned.

When the pasta is al dente, drain and put into a warmed deep bowl. Pour in the prosciutto and pan contents and toss the pasta to coat all strands. Add the cheese, salt and pepper to the eggs and pour over the pasta. Mix well and serve.

4 to 6 servings.

Maruzzelle with Turnip Greens

1	pound turnip greens	1	teaspoon salt
1	pound maruzzelle	¼	teaspoon pepper
4	tablespoons oil	¼	teaspoon dried oregano
2	cloves garlic, minced		leaves

Wash the turnip greens in several changes of water until clean. Put into a pot without drying the leaves and boil, covered, for about 12 minutes or until almost tender.

While the greens are cooking, put the pasta on to cook, following package directions.

Heat the oil in a 10- to 12-inch skillet over medium heat. Add the garlic and cook, stirring, until golden.

Drain the pasta just before it is al dente and add to the skillet along with the cooked turnip greens and the pot juices, the salt, pepper and oregano. Mix well and simmer for 3 to 5 minutes. Serve hot.

4 to 6 servings.

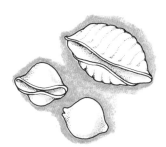

Maruzzine with Potatoes and Basil

4	tablespoons oil	¼	teaspoon dried oregano
4	medium potatoes, peeled and diced		leaves
2	small onions, finely chopped	2	tablespoons chopped fresh basil leaves or 2 teaspoons dried basil leaves
2	cloves garlic, minced	2	tablespoons chopped parsley
1	can (16 ounces) tomato sauce	1	pound maruzzine
1	teaspoon salt	½	cup grated Romano cheese
¼	teaspoon pepper		

> **Maruzzelle and maruzzine are, respectively, medium and small shells. Maruzze are the large shells. Cavatelli, rotelle and riccini make good substitutes.**

Heat the oil in a heavy 8-inch skillet. Add the potatoes, onions and garlic. Cook, stirring frequently, until the onions are transparent. Add the tomato sauce and remaining ingredients except the pasta and cheese. Cover and cook over low heat for about 20 minutes or until the potatoes are tender.

Cook the pasta according to package directions until al dente. Drain and put into a warmed deep bowl. Stir in the potato mixture. Serve with grated cheese on the side.

4 to 6 servings.

Baked Maruzzine with Cauliflower

1 pound maruzzine, cooked and rinsed in cold water	1 teaspoon salt
	¼ teaspoon pepper
1 small head cauliflower, separated into flowerets, cooked and drained	¼ teaspoon dried oregano leaves
	¼ teaspoon garlic powder
4 tablespoons butter, melted	½ cup shredded mozzarella cheese
½ cup grated Romano cheese	

Combine the cooked pasta and cauliflower in a shallow baking dish. Pour the melted butter on top and sprinkle with the grated Romano, salt, pepper, oregano and garlic powder. Toss to mix and then sprinkle with the shredded mozzarella. Bake in a preheated 375° oven for 10 minutes or until the mozzarella is melted.

4 to 6 servings.

Mostaccioli, or mustaches, are long tubes that also come ridged as mostaccioli rigati. Use ziti, mezzani or mezzani rigati as substitutes.

Mostaccioli with Bracciole

1-pound slice round steak, about ½ inch thick	4 tablespoons oil
	2 small onions, minced
2 hard-boiled eggs, chopped	1 clove garlic, minced
3 slices bacon, chopped	1 can (29 ounces) tomato puree
½ cup dry bread crumbs	
¼ cup grated Romano cheese	1 pound mostaccioli
½ teaspoon salt	½ cup grated Romano cheese
¼ teaspoon pepper	
¼ teaspoon dried oregano leaves	

Score the steak lightly on both sides and spread out on a flat surface. Mix the hard-boiled eggs, bacon, bread crumbs, ¼ cup grated Romano cheese, salt, pepper and oregano in a bowl. Spread over the steak. Roll and tie with string to hold the filling in.

Heat the oil in a casserole large enough to hold the rolled steak. Add the onions and garlic. Cook over medium-high heat, stirring, until the onions are transparent. Add the rolled steak and brown on all sides. Pour the tomato puree over the steak and bring to a boil. Cover and bake in a preheated 375° oven for 2 hours.

Cook the pasta according to package directions until al dente. Drain and put onto a warmed platter.

Remove the bracciole from the casserole and pour the sauce in it over the pasta. Sprinkle with the ½ cup grated Romano. Cut the bracciole into 1-inch slices. Arrange them on top of the pasta and sauce. Serve hot.

4 to 6 servings.

Baked Noodles Italian Style

4 cups tomato sauce	2 cups shredded mozzarella
1 pound noodles, cooked and	cheese
rinsed in cold water	½ cup grated Romano cheese

Spread about ½ cup of the tomato sauce in the bottom of a 13½x9x2-inch baking dish. Cover with ⅓ of the pasta and sprinkle with ½ cup mozzarella. Repeat the layers. Put the remaining pasta on top and cover with the rest of the sauce. Sprinkle on the remaining mozzarella and then the Romano. Cover firmly with aluminum foil and bake in a preheated 375° oven for 25 to 30 minutes. Serve hot.

4 to 6 servings.

■ Substitute 4 cups Béchamel sauce (page 30) for the tomato sauce and give this recipe a new complexion.

Noodles with Tuna and Anchovy Sauce

4 tablespoons butter	1 can (7 ounces) tuna,
4 tablespoons oil	drained and flaked
2 small onions, finely	1 can (2 ounces) anchovy
chopped	fillets, drained
2 cloves garlic, minced	1 can (4 ounces) pitted black
1 pound mushrooms, sliced	olives, drained
½ teaspoon salt	1 pound noodles
¼ teaspoon pepper	½ cup grated Romano cheese

Melt the butter in the oil in a heavy 8-inch skillet over medium heat. Add the onions and garlic and cook, stirring occasionally, until the onions are transparent. Add the mushrooms and continue cooking, stirring from time to time, for about 10 minutes. Add the salt, pepper, tuna and anchovies. Simmer for 5 minutes. Stir in the olives a minute or two before serving.

While the sauce is simmering, cook the pasta according to package directions until al dente. Drain and place in a warmed deep bowl. Add the sauce and mix gently. Sprinkle with the cheese and serve.

4 to 6 servings.

Noodles are ribbon-shaped pasta that, unlike other pastas, usually contain eggs. They vary in width from the very narrow soup noodles to the extra-wide lasagne noodles. Some are wavy (mafalde and margherite), some are curly (cavatelli) and some are pinched into bowties. When made with spinach, they are green.

Green Noodles with Shrimp

1 pound green noodles
8 tablespoons butter
5 tablespoons oil
1 pound raw shrimp, shelled, deveined and cut into halves

1 teaspoon salt
¼ teaspoon pepper
2 cloves garlic, minced
½ cup heavy cream, heated

Put the pasta on to cook, following package directions.

While the pasta is cooking, melt the butter in the oil in a heavy 8-inch skillet over high heat. Add the shrimp, salt, pepper and garlic and cook, stirring, for several minutes until the shrimp are a bright pink.

When the pasta is al dente, drain and put into a warmed deep bowl. Add the shrimp mixture and heated cream to the pasta and toss gently. Serve hot.

4 to 6 servings.

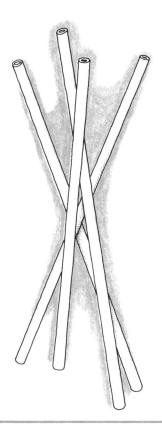

Perciatelli with Eggplant and Green Olive Sauce

4 tablespoons oil
2 cloves garlic, minced
2½ cups tomato sauce
1 teaspoon salt
¼ teaspoon pepper
¼ teaspoon dried oregano leaves
2 tablespoons chopped fresh basil leaves

½ cup pitted green olives, chopped
1 small eggplant (about 1 pound), peeled and diced
1 pound perciatelli
½ cup grated Romano cheese

Heat the oil in a heavy 8-inch skillet over medium heat. Add the garlic. Cook, stirring as needed, until the garlic is golden. Add the tomato sauce, seasonings and green olives. Bring to a boil, lower heat and simmer, uncovered, for 20 minutes. Add the eggplant and simmer for about 15 minutes or until the eggplant is tender.

While the eggplant is simmering, cook the pasta according to package directions until al dente. Drain and place on a warmed platter. Pour the sauce over the pasta and mix gently. Sprinkle with cheese and serve hot.

4 to 6 servings.

Although perciatelli is made in long spaghetti-like strands, it is called thin macaroni because there's a hole in it. It's larger than bucatini and smaller than maccaroncelli, either of which can be used in its place, as can also spaghetti.

Perciatelli with Pork Hocks

4 tablespoons oil	1 cup dry white wine
2 medium onions, finely	1 bay leaf
chopped	1 teaspoon dried basil
2 cloves garlic, minced	leaves
6 fresh pork hocks	1 teaspoon salt
1 can (28 ounces) plum	¼ teaspoon pepper
tomatoes	¼ teaspoon dried oregano
1 can (6 ounces) tomato	leaves
paste	1 pound perciatelli
1 can (6 ounces) water	
(use tomato paste can)	

Heat the oil in a heavy deep pot over medium heat. Add the onions, garlic and pork hocks. Cook, stirring frequently, for 10 minutes. Add the tomatoes, crushing them in your hand as you add them, and the liquid from the can. Add the remaining ingredients except the pasta. Bring to a boil, lower heat and simmer, uncovered, for 2½ to 3 hours or until the pork hocks are tender. Stir occasionally to avoid burning.

Cook the pasta according to package directions until al dente. Drain and place on a warmed platter. Pour about 2 cups of the sauce over the pasta and mix well. Place the ham hocks on top and serve with the extra sauce on the side.

4 to 6 servings.

Riccini with Zucchini in Basil Sauce

1 pound riccini	2 cups milk
4 tablespoons oil	½ cup fresh basil leaves,
3 medium zucchini, sliced	finely chopped
into ¼-inch rounds	1 teaspoon salt
2 tablespoons butter	2 eggs, well beaten
3 tablespoons flour	½ cup grated Romano cheese

Put the pasta on to cook, following package directions.

Heat the oil in a heavy 10- to 12-inch skillet over medium heat. Add the zucchini slices and fry until lightly colored. Drain the oil from the pan.

Melt the butter in a saucepan. Stir in the flour and add the milk gradually, stirring to avoid lumps. Add the basil and salt and stir to mix. Remove from heat and stir in the eggs and cheese.

When the pasta is al dente, drain it. Add to the zucchini and stir in the sauce. Serve hot.

4 to 6 servings.

Riccini are delightful little curls. If it's shape you are looking for, cavatelli, rotelle, shells or spaghetti twists can be substituted.

Rotelle and Italian Meatballs

4 cups tomato sauce	1 pound rotelle
Italian Meatballs (below)	½ cup grated Romano cheese

Prepare the sauce and the meatballs. About 5 minutes before serving, add the meatballs to the sauce to warm through.

Cook the pasta according to package directions until al dente. Drain and put onto a warmed platter and mix with about 2 cups of the sauce. Sprinkle with the cheese and place the meatballs on top. Serve with the remaining sauce and additional grated cheese.

4 to 6 servings.

Italian Meatballs

½ pound ground beef	2 tablespoons chopped parsley
¼ pound ground veal	2 cloves garlic, minced
¼ pound ground pork	1½ teaspoons salt
4 slices stale bread, soaked in water, squeezed dry and torn into pieces	¼ teaspoon pepper
	⅛ teaspoon dried oregano leaves
3 eggs	½ teaspoon fennel seed
½ cup grated Romano cheese	

Place the meats in a large bowl and add the bread. Add the remaining ingredients and mix well, but lightly, with your hands. Oil your hands and form the mixture into 12 balls. Put onto a shallow baking pan and place in a preheated 375° oven for 25 to 30 minutes or until the meatballs are browned and cooked through.

This recipe makes about 10 to 12 large balls, 30 medium balls or 50 small balls. Cook the medium balls for about 18 minutes and the small balls about 12 minutes.

Paesano Pie

1 can (8 ounces) tomato sauce	2 cloves garlic, minced
	1 teaspoon salt
1 pound ground beef	¼ teaspoon pepper
2 eggs	¼ teaspoon dried oregano leaves
½ cup dry bread crumbs	
1 small onion, finely chopped	Paesano Filling (right)
1 small green pepper, seeded and finely chopped	½ cup shredded mozzarella cheese

Combine all ingredients except the filling and the mozzarella in a large bowl and mix well. Pat into a greased 10-inch pie plate, covering the bottom and side evenly.

Prepare the filling and pour into the pie plate. Sprinkle with the mozzarella and cover firmly with aluminum foil. Bake in a preheated 375° oven for 35 minutes. Remove the foil and continue cooking for 15 minutes more. Serve hot.

4 to 6 servings.

Paesano Filling

½ pound seme mellone
 cooked and rinsed
 in cold water
1 can (16 ounces) tomato
 sauce
½ teaspoon salt

¼ teaspoon pepper
¼ teaspoon dried oregano
 leaves
¼ teaspoon garlic powder
½ cup grated Romano cheese

Combine ingredients in a bowl and stir well.

Eggplant Stuffed with Seme Mellone

2 small eggplants
 (about 1 pound each)
½ pound ground beef
½ pound ground pork
½ pound seme mellone,
 cooked and rinsed in
 cold water
3 eggs
1 teaspoon salt

¼ teaspoon pepper
¼ teaspoon dried oregano
 leaves
¼ teaspoon garlic powder
2 teaspoons chopped parsley
½ cup grated Romano cheese
2 cups tomato sauce
½ cup shredded mozzarella
 cheese

Seme mellone (melon seeds) are a soup pasta. Use acini pepe (peppercorns), stelline (stars), or any other soup pasta in their place.

Cut eggplants in half lengthwise. Carefully scoop out the pulp with a grapefruit knife, leaving the skins intact. Cut the pulp into small cubes.

In a large mixing bowl, combine the meats, pasta, eggs, salt, pepper, oregano, garlic powder, parsley, Romano cheese and cubed eggplant. Mix well. Mound the eggplant shells with the mixture. Place in a baking pan and pour the tomato sauce over all. Cover the pan firmly with aluminum foil. Bake in a preheated 375° oven for 1 hour. Uncover and sprinkle mozzarella cheese over the eggplants. Bake for 5 minutes longer or until the cheese is melted. Serve hot.

4 servings.

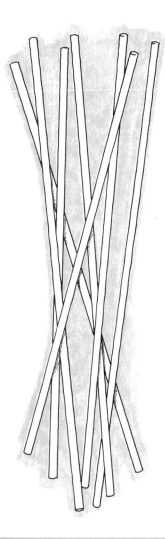

Spaghetti and Tuna Casserole

1 pound spaghetti	1 teaspoon salt
3 hard-boiled eggs, sliced	¼ teaspoon pepper
1 can (7 ounces) tuna, drained and flaked	¼ teaspoon dried oregano leaves
1 can (17 ounces) peas, drained	¼ teaspoon garlic powder
½ cup grated Romano cheese	1¼ cups milk
	2 tablespoons butter

Break the pasta into small pieces and cook according to package directions until just al dente. Drain in a colander and run under cold water. Put ⅓ of the pasta into a greased 3-quart casserole. Cover with ½ of the eggs, tuna and peas and sprinkle with 2 tablespoons of the cheese. Repeat. Cover with the remaining pasta and sprinkle with the remaining cheese. Add the seasonings to the milk and heat. Pour over the pasta and dot with the butter. Bake, uncovered, in a preheated 375° oven for 15 to 20 minutes.

4 to 6 servings.

Spaghetti and Cabbage Stew

1 small head cabbage, cut into chunks	1 cup drained canned tomatoes, crushed
4 tablespoons oil	1 teaspoon salt
1 large onion, thinly sliced	¼ teaspoon pepper
2 cloves garlic, minced	¼ teaspoon dried oregano leaves
1 package (10 ounces) frozen mixed vegetables, partially thawed and broken apart	¼ cup grated Romano cheese
	½ pound spaghetti

Drop the cabbage into a pan of boiling water and cook for about 20 minutes or until tender; drain.

Heat the oil in a heavy 10- to 12-inch skillet over medium heat. Add the onion and garlic. Cook, stirring occasionally, until the onion is transparent. Add the cooked cabbage, mixed vegetables and tomatoes. Season with the salt, pepper and oregano. Sprinkle with cheese and simmer for 30 minutes.

Cook the pasta according to package directions until al dente. Drain and toss with the cabbage stew. Serve hot.

4 servings.

■ This is an old D'Agostino family favorite.

> **Spaghetti is made of solid strands of pasta. Macaroni is hollow and may be long or short. Both are round, while noodles are flat. Spaghetti and macaroni are what most folks reach for on their grocery shelves, but any of these spaghetti recipes can be made with almost any pasta you choose.**

Spaghetti with Chicken Livers and Mushrooms

4 cups tomato sauce	1 pound chicken livers
1 pound spaghetti	¾ pound mushrooms, sliced
4 tablespoons butter	Grated Romano cheese

Prepare the tomato sauce. When it is almost done, put the pasta on to cook, following package directions.

Melt the butter in a heavy skillet over medium-high heat. Add the chicken livers and mushrooms. Cook, stirring, until the livers are browned. Add the livers and mushrooms to the sauce and simmer until the pasta is ready.

When the pasta is al dente, drain and put onto a warmed platter. Toss with about 2 cups of the sauce and top with the chicken livers. Serve with the remaining sauce and the grated cheese on the side.

4 to 6 servings.

Spaghetti with Artichoke Sauce

½ cup oil	1 teaspoon salt
2 small onions, finely chopped	½ teaspoon pepper
2 cloves garlic, minced	¼ teaspoon dried oregano leaves
½ pound mushrooms, sliced	1 can (28 ounces) plum tomatoes
1 package (9 ounces) frozen artichoke hearts, partially thawed and broken apart	1 pound spaghetti
	½ cup grated Parmesan cheese

Heat the oil in a heavy 10- to 12-inch skillet over medium heat. Add the onions, garlic, mushrooms and artichoke hearts. Cook, stirring as needed, for 10 minutes. Sprinkle with the seasonings. Add the tomatoes, crushing them in your hand as you add them, and the liquid from the can. Bring to a boil, lower heat and simmer, uncovered, for 1 hour.

When the sauce is almost done, cook the pasta according to package directions until al dente. Drain and put onto a warmed platter. Mix with about 2 cups of the sauce. Serve with the remaining sauce and the cheese on the side.

4 to 6 servings.

Spaghetti alla Carbonara

4 tablespoons oil
½ pound bacon, cut into small
    pieces
2 cloves garlic, minced
¼ teaspoon pepper
¼ teaspoon dried oregano
    leaves

1 pound spaghetti
3 eggs, beaten
½ cup grated Romano cheese
¼ cup shredded mozzarella
    cheese

Heat the oil in a heavy 8-inch skillet over medium heat. Add the bacon, garlic, pepper and oregano. Cook, stirring as needed, until the garlic is golden and the bacon is on the crisp side. Remove from heat.

While the sauce is cooking, boil the pasta according to package directions until just al dente. Drain and put onto a heatproof platter. Gently stir in the eggs, then the bacon sauce and Romano cheese. Sprinkle with the mozzarella and place under the broiler for a few minutes or until the cheese is melted but not browned.

4 to 6 servings.

> **Al dente means firm to the tooth, and that's how pasta should be cooked. The only sure way of testing pasta is to bite it. Keep trying until it's done just the way you like it. Just don't cook it so long that it's mushy.**

Spaghetti with Mama D's White Clam Sauce

4 tablespoons oil
1 large onion, chopped
2 cloves garlic, minced
1 can (8 ounces) minced
    clams
1 tablespoon chopped parsley

½ teaspoon pepper
¼ teaspoon dried oregano
    leaves
1 cup bottled clam juice
1 pound spaghetti
¼ cup grated Romano cheese

Heat the oil in a heavy 8-inch skillet over medium heat. Add the onion and garlic. Cook, stirring as needed, until the onion is transparent. Add the clams, liquid and all, and the remaining ingredients except the pasta and cheese. Bring to a boil. Reduce heat and simmer, uncovered, for about 30 minutes.

While the sauce is simmering, cook the pasta according to package directions until al dente. Drain and place on a warmed platter. Sprinkle with the cheese. Top with the clam sauce and serve immediately.

4 to 6 servings.

■ I know cheese isn't supposed to be served with clam sauce, but my customers love it. If you want to follow the rules, leave it out.

Mama D's Spaghetti with Ricotta

1 pound spaghetti	⅛ teaspoon dried oregano
1 cup ricotta cheese	leaves
¼ cup grated Parmesan	⅛ teaspoon garlic powder
cheese	4 tablespoons butter
1 egg, beaten	¼ cup shredded mozzarella
½ teaspoon salt	cheese
¼ teaspoon pepper	

Put the pasta on to cook, following package directions.

While the pasta is cooking, combine the ricotta cheese with the Parmesan, egg, salt, pepper, oregano and garlic powder. Taste for seasoning.

When the pasta is just al dente, drain, leaving a little water in the pot. Add the butter to the pot and return the pasta to it, tossing well. Stir in the ricotta cheese mixture and put into a baking dish. Top with the shredded mozzarella and put under the broiler until the mozzarella is melted but not browned.

4 to 6 servings.

■ A most pleasant and wonderfully creamy taste.

> **I am not usually fussy about the kind of oil I use. Any good vegetable oil will do, and if it is on sale, so much the better. But in this dish, where the oil is the sauce, use a good olive oil.**

Spaghetti with Garlic and Oil Sauce

½ cup olive oil	¼ teaspoon pepper
4 cloves garlic, crushed	½ cup dry bread crumbs
1 teaspoon dried basil leaves	1 pound spaghetti
1 teaspoon salt	½ cup grated Romano cheese

Heat the oil in a heavy 8-inch skillet until the oil is very hot but not smoking. Add the garlic and cook until lightly browned but not burned. Discard the garlic. Add the basil, salt, pepper and bread crumbs and stir. Turn heat to low and brown the crumbs for several minutes.

Cook the pasta according to package directions until al dente. Drain and place on a warmed large platter. Pour the oil mixture over the pasta, stirring gently. Sprinkle with the grated cheese and serve hot.

4 to 6 servings.

> **Putting garlic through a press only pulverizes it. If you want to crush garlic, put it on a board and give it a whack with the broad side of a cleaver.**

Spaghetti with Shrimp

1 pound spaghetti	¼ teaspoon pepper
½ cup oil	¼ teaspoon dried oregano
2 small onions	leaves
2 cloves garlic, minced	1 pound raw shrimp, shelled
2 tablespoons chopped	and deveined (left whole
parsley	or cut into pieces)
1 teaspoon salt	

Put the pasta on to cook, following package directions.

While the pasta is cooking, heat the oil in a heavy 10- to 12-inch skillet over medium-high heat. Add the onions, garlic, parsley, salt, pepper and oregano. Cook, stirring, until the onions are transparent. Add the shrimp and cook, stirring occasionally, for 5 to 6 minutes or until the shrimp are pink.

When the pasta is al dente, drain and put into a warmed deep bowl. Toss with the shrimp mixture and serve immediately.

4 to 6 servings.

Spaghetti with Zucchini

2 tablespoons butter	¼ teaspoon pepper
2 tablespoons oil	¼ teaspoon dried oregano
2 small onions, finely	leaves
chopped	2 cups tomato sauce
2 cloves garlic, minced	1 pound spaghetti
4 medium zucchini, sliced	½ cup grated Romano cheese
1 teaspoon dried basil leaves	½ cup shredded mozzarella
1 teaspoon salt	cheese

Melt the butter in the oil in a heavy 10- to 12-inch skillet over medium high heat. Add the onions, garlic, zucchini and seasonings. Cook, stirring, until the garlic and zucchini are golden but not burned. Add the tomato sauce and heat just to boiling.

Cook the pasta according to package directions until just al dente. Drain and stir into the zucchini mixture with the grated Romano cheese.

Pour the contents of the skillet into a baking dish. Sprinkle with the mozzarella cheese and put into a preheated 375° oven for 10 minutes or until the cheese is melted and lightly browned. Serve at once.

4 to 6 servings.

> **The package directions on store-bought pastas usually tell you to cook them longer than you should if you like your pasta al dente. Start testing the pasta a minute or two before the box says. Bite into a piece and take the pot off the heat if you think the pasta's done.**

Marinated Spaghetti

½ cup oil
½ cup grated Romano cheese
1 cup pitted green olives
½ cup finely chopped onion
2 cloves garlic, minced
1 teaspoon salt
¼ teaspoon pepper

¼ teaspoon dried oregano
  leaves
1 cup diced boiled potatoes
1 cup cubed mozzarella
  cheese
1 pound spaghetti

Mix the oil, Romano cheese, olives, onion, garlic, salt, pepper, oregano, potatoes and mozzarella in a bowl large enough to hold the pasta. Marinate for 1 hour at room temperature.

Cook the pasta according to package directions until al dente. Drain and add to the bowl with the sauce. Mix well and serve.

4 to 6 servings.

Spaghetti with Seafood Sauce

4 tablespoons olive oil
1 medium onion, finely
  chopped
3 cloves garlic, chopped
2 cans (35 ounces each)
  plum tomatoes, coarsely
  chopped and liquid
  reserved
2 cans (6 ounces each)
  tomato paste

2 cans (2 ounces each)
  anchovy fillets
1 can (12¾ ounces) tuna
  packed in oil
12 little neck clams, well
  scrubbed
½ pound shrimp, shelled and
  deveined
2 pounds spaghetti
  Grated Romano cheese

Heat the oil in a Dutch oven over medium heat. Add the onion and garlic. Cook, stirring occasionally, until they are golden brown but not burned. Add the chopped tomatoes and cook for 5 minutes. Add the reserved canned tomato liquid and cook an additional 5 minutes. Stir in the tomato paste and let bubble, uncovered, over medium heat for 45 minutes, stirring occasionally.

Chop the anchovies and flake the tuna, reserving the oil in both cans. Add, oil and all, to the sauce and cook for 5 minutes. Add the clams and shrimp and cook until the clam shells open.

Cook the pasta according to package directions until al dente. Drain and place on a warmed large platter. Mix with 4 cups of the sauce. Place the clams in their shells on top and serve with the remaining sauce and the grated cheese on the side.

8 to 12 servings.

> **When browning garlic, be sure you don't burn it. Burnt garlic has a harsh, disagreeable taste that can ruin the whole dish.**

Spaghetti with Herb Sauce

1 pound spaghetti	3 tablespoons finely chopped fresh basil leaves
1 cup butter	½ teaspoon salt
3 tablespoons lemon juice	¼ teaspoon pepper
1 cup finely chopped parsley	1 cup grated Parmesan cheese
3 tablespoons finely chopped fresh mint leaves	

Put the pasta on to cook, following package directions.

While the pasta is cooking, melt the butter in a heavy 8-inch skillet until sizzling. Add the lemon juice, herbs and seasonings and mix.

When the pasta is al dente, drain and put into a warmed deep bowl. Toss with the sauce and then with half the cheese. Serve hot with the remaining cheese on the side.

4 to 6 servings.

Spaghettini with Cod and Black Olive Sauce

4 tablespoons oil	1 teaspoon salt
2 onions, finely chopped	¼ teaspoon pepper
2 cloves garlic, minced	⅛ teaspoon dried oregano leaves
1½ pounds cod fillets, cut into pieces	1 bay leaf
1 can (28 ounces) plum tomatoes	1 pound spaghettini
2 cans (8 ounces each) pitted black olives, drained	½ cup grated Romano cheese

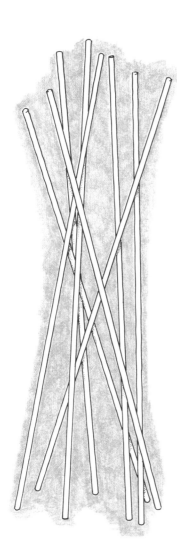

Heat the oil in a heavy 10- to 12-inch skillet over medium heat. Add the onions and garlic. Cook, stirring, until the onions are transparent. Add the cod and cook, stirring, for 3 to 5 minutes.

Add the tomatoes, crushing them in your hand as you add them, and the liquid from the can. Stir in the remaining ingredients except the pasta and cheese. Bring to a boil. Lower heat and simmer, uncovered, for about 2 hours.

Cook the pasta according to package directions until al dente. Drain and place on a warmed platter. Spoon the sauce over the pasta, sprinkle with the cheese and serve.

4 to 6 servings.

Spaghettini is thinner than spaghetti, thicker than vermicelli. I find it a pleasant change from spaghetti.

Vermicelli with John's Crab and Shrimp Sauce

4 tablespoons oil
1 small onion, finely chopped
4 cloves garlic, minced
  Pinch of dried oregano leaves
  Pinch of dried basil leaves
2 tablespoons chopped parsley
1 pound unshelled shrimp, split down the back

1 package (6 ounces) frozen Alaska king crabmeat, partially thawed and broken into pieces
1 can (28 ounces) plum tomatoes, drained
1 pound vermicelli

Heat the oil in a heavy 10- to 12-inch skillet over medium heat. Add the onion, garlic, oregano, basil, parsley, shrimp and crabmeat. Cook, stirring, for 5 minutes. Squeeze the tomatoes into the pan with your hand and cook, uncovered, over medium heat for about 30 minutes. Cook the pasta according to package directions until al dente. Drain and put onto a warmed platter. Serve with the sauce on top.

4 to 6 servings.

Ziti with Anchovy and Olive Sauce

4 tablespoons oil
2 medium onions, chopped
2 cloves garlic, minced
1 can (2 ounces) anchovy fillets
1 can (28 ounces) plum tomatoes
½ cup chopped pimiento-stuffed green olives

½ cup chopped black olives
2 tablespoons chopped capers
1 teaspoon dried basil leaves
½ teaspoon salt
½ teaspoon pepper
¼ teaspoon dried oregano leaves
1 pound ziti

Heat the oil in an 10- to 12-inch heavy skillet. Add the onions, garlic and anchovies with their oil. Cook, stirring, over medium heat until the onions are transparent. Add the tomatoes, crushing them in your hand as you add them, and the liquid from the can. Stir in the remaining ingredients except the pasta. Bring to a boil. Lower the heat and simmer for about 2 hours. Cook the pasta according to package directions until al dente. Drain and put into a warmed deep bowl. Stir in the sauce.

4 to 6 servings.

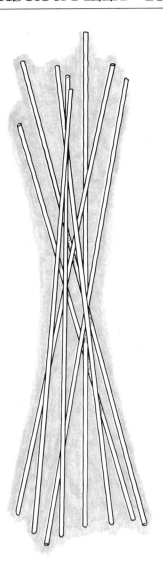

Vermicelli is the thinnest form of spaghetti. It is also made in clusters, called fidelini.

Ziti are large tubes of macaroni. Good substitutes are the smaller mezzani, maccaroncelli, mostaccioli and the ridged mezzani rigati and mostaccioli rigati.

Baked Ziti
with Mushrooms and Sausage

1 pound sweet or hot Italian sausage Topping (below)	¼ teaspoon pepper ¼ teaspoon dried oregano leaves
1 pound ziti	¼ teaspoon garlic powder
1 can (8 ounces) sliced mushrooms, drained	2 cups tomato sauce ½ cup shredded mozzarella
½ cup grated Romano cheese	cheese
1 teaspoon salt	

Place the sausage in a shallow baking pan and bake in a preheated 375° oven for 40 minutes or until the sausage is browned and cooked through. Cut into ¼-inch pieces. Prepare the topping.

Cook the pasta according to package directions until just al dente. Drain and place in a mixing bowl. Add the sliced sausage, mushrooms, Romano, salt, pepper, oregano and garlic powder to the bowl. Mix with 1 cup of the tomato sauce. Transfer to baking pan and pour the remaining sauce on top. Sprinkle with the bread crumb topping.

Bake, uncovered, in a preheated 375° oven for 45 minutes. Sprinkle with the mozzarella and return to the oven for 10 minutes or until the cheese is melted.

4 to 6 servings.

Topping

1 cup dry bread crumbs	¼ teaspoon dried oregano leaves
½ cup grated Romano cheese	¼ teaspoon garlic powder
½ teaspoon salt	2 teaspoons chopped parsley
¼ teaspoon pepper	

Combine all ingredients and mix well.

Bean and Bacon Soup

1 pound Great Northern beans	1 teaspoon dried basil leaves
4 quarts water	2 tablespoons chopped parsley
2 tablespoons oil	1 tablespoon salt
2 medium onions, finely chopped	2 medium potatoes, peeled and diced
2 cloves garlic, minced	3 stalks celery, chopped
½ pound bacon, cut into small pieces	3 carrots, sliced
¼ teaspoon pepper	1 cup tubettini, cooked and rinsed in cold water
¼ teaspoon dried oregano leaves	Grated Romano cheese

Wash the beans thoroughly and put in a bowl with water to cover by a few inches; soak overnight. Put the beans and the water they soaked in into a 6- to 8-quart pot. Add the 4 quarts water and bring to a boil. Lower heat and simmer the beans, covered, for 1 hour.

While the beans are cooking, heat the oil in a heavy 8-inch skillet over medium heat. Add the onions, garlic and bacon and cook, stirring, until the onions are transparent. Add the pepper, oregano, basil and parsley.

Replace the water lost in the bean pot during cooking and add the salt and the potatoes, celery and carrots. Bring the liquid to a boil. Add the onion mixture. Reduce the heat and simmer, partially covered, for 2 hours.

Add the cooked pasta and simmer for 2 to 3 minutes. Serve the soup in large bowls and sprinkle with grated cheese. The soup should be very hot.

8 to 10 servings.

> When pasta isn't served as a separate course at an Italian meal, then it's literally in the soup—hot, rib-sticking soup that with a salad makes a meal.

Lentil and Bacon Soup

1 cup lentils	1 tablespoon finely chopped parsley
2 quarts cold water	
1 tablespoon salt	1 teaspoon salt
4 tablespoons oil	¼ teaspoon pepper
4 slices bacon, cut into small pieces	¼ teaspoon dried oregano leaves
2 small onions, finely chopped	1 can (28 ounces) plum tomatoes
2 cloves garlic, minced	1 cup ditalini

Wash the lentils and put in a 4-quart pot. Add the water and the 1 tablespoon salt. Bring to a boil, lower heat and simmer, covered, for about 1 hour or until lentils are tender.

Heat the oil in a heavy 10- to 12-inch skillet over medium heat. Add the bacon, onions and garlic and cook, stirring, until the bacon is done but not crisp. Stir in the parsley, the 1 teaspoon salt, pepper and oregano. Add the tomatoes, crushing them in your hand as you add them, and the liquid from the can. Bring to a boil. Lower heat and simmer, uncovered, for 30 minutes.

When the lentils are done, stir the tomato mixture and pasta into the soup pot. Cook until the pasta is al dente.

4 to 6 servings.

Vegetable-Bean Soup

Cannellini are white kidney beans, much favored in the Italian kitchen. They come canned but when you can't find them, use Great Northern beans instead.

2 quarts beef broth	2 medium potatoes, peeled and diced
1 can (20 ounces) cannellini	
1 can (16 ounces) chick peas	2 medium zucchini, sliced
3 stalks celery with leaves, chopped	2 cups chopped cabbage
	1 cup tubetti
3 carrots, sliced	½ cup grated Romano cheese

Heat the broth to boiling in a large pot. Add the beans, chick peas and vegetables. Lower heat and cook slowly, covered, for about 20 minutes.

Toward the end of the cooking time, bring the soup to a boil and add the pasta. Cook, uncovered, until the pasta is al dente. Remove from heat and stir in the cheese. Serve immediately.

6 servings.

Potato-Zucchini Soup

1 tablespoon butter	¼ cup grated Romano cheese
2 tablespoons oil	
2 medium potatoes, peeled and diced	2 tablespoons chopped parsley
4 medium zucchini, diced	1 tablespoon chopped fresh basil leaves
1½ quarts beef broth or water	
½ cup tubetti	3 eggs

Melt the butter in the oil in a heavy 3-quart pot over medium heat. Add the potatoes and zucchini and cook, stirring, until the vegetables are lightly browned. Add the beef broth (if using water instead of broth, add 1 teaspoon salt and ¼ teaspoon pepper). Bring the liquid to a boil. Lower the heat and simmer, covered, for about 20 minutes or until the potatoes are done.

Bring the soup to a boil; add the pasta and cook until al dente.

Add the cheese, parsley and basil to the eggs and whisk well with a fork. When the soup is done, remove from the heat and with a fork stir in the egg mixture until well blended. Serve hot.

4 to 6 servings.

> **Tubettini are the smallest of the short pasta tubes. They are followed, in order of increasing size, by tubetti, ditalini and ditali. The larger the size, the more prominent in your soup.**

Broccoli Soup with Tubettini

½ pound salt pork, diced	1 teaspoon salt
3 tablespoons oil	¼ teaspoon pepper
2 onions, finely chopped	1 package (10 ounces) frozen broccoli
2 cloves garlic, minced	
1 can (6 ounces) tomato paste	1 cup tubettini
	½ cup grated Romano cheese
2 quarts water	

Brown the salt pork in a heavy 4-quart pot over medium heat. Drain the fat and add the oil, onions, garlic, tomato paste, water, salt and pepper. Bring to a boil and cook for 25 minutes. Add the broccoli and pasta and cook for 10 minutes longer. Serve hot in bowls and sprinkle with Romano cheese.

6 servings.

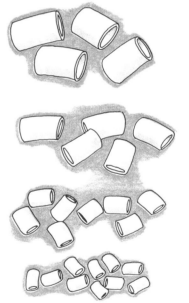

Spring Soup

2 tablespoons butter
2 tablespoons oil
1 small onion, chopped
2 cloves garlic, minced
2 tablespoons chopped parsley
4 ripe tomatoes, seeded and chopped
1½ teaspoons salt
¼ teaspoon pepper
¼ teaspoon dried oregano leaves
2 quarts beef broth or chicken broth
2 stalks celery, sliced
2 medium zucchini, sliced
2 carrots, sliced
2 potatoes, peeled and diced
1 package (10 ounces) frozen artichoke hearts, thawed and cut into chunks
1 can (17 ounces) peas
1 pound orzo, cooked and rinsed in cold water
½ cup grated Romano cheese

Melt the butter in the oil in a heavy skillet or saucepan over medium heat. Add the onion, garlic and parsley. Cook, stirring, until onion is transparent. Add the tomatoes, salt, pepper and oregano. Lower heat and simmer for about 15 minutes.

Heat the broth to boiling in a large pot. Add the remaining vegetables and the tomato mixture from the skillet. Cover and cook slowly for 20 minutes or until vegetables are tender. Add the pasta and stir in the grated cheese until thoroughly mixed.

8 servings.

Orzo resembles rice more than it does barley, for which it is named. Use acini pepe, tubettini, seme mellone or any other soup pasta.

Minestrone, Tuscan Style

1 pound Great Northern beans
4 quarts water
½ cup oil
2 onions, coarsely chopped
4 cloves garlic, minced
2 tablespoons chopped parsley
½ teaspoon salt
¼ teaspoon pepper
3 or 4 ripe tomatoes, coarsely chopped
4 stalks celery, sliced
4 carrots, diced
2 medium potatoes, peeled and diced
1 can (16 ounces) chick peas
1 tablespoon chopped parsley
1 tablespoon salt
¼ teaspoon pepper
1 medium zucchini, diced
1 cup maruzzine

Wash the beans thoroughly and put in a bowl with water to cover by a few inches; soak overnight. Put the beans and the water they soaked in into a 6- to 8-quart pot. Add the 4 quarts water and bring to a boil. Lower heat and simmer the beans, covered, for 1 hour.

I don't usually seed tomatoes, but it's easy enough to do. Cut the tomato in half crosswise, then squeeze the halves, forcing the seeds out.

While the beans are cooking, heat the oil in a heavy 8-inch skillet over medium heat. Add the onions, garlic, 2 tablespoons chopped parsley, ½ teaspoon salt and ¼ teaspoon pepper. Cook, stirring as needed, until the onions are golden brown. Reduce heat to medium-low, add the tomatoes and cook, uncovered, for about 20 to 30 minutes or until the tomatoes are reduced.

Replace the water lost in the bean pot during the cooking and add the tomato mixture along with the celery, carrots, potatoes, chick peas with their liquid, and the 1 tablespoon chopped parsley, 1 tablespoon salt and ¼ teaspoon pepper. Simmer, covered, for 1 hour.

About 10 minutes before the end of the cooking time, bring the soup to a boil. Add the zucchini and pasta. Cook until the pasta is al dente.

8 to 10 servings.

Minestrone, Genoese Style

4 tablespoons oil	2 quarts water
2 medium onions, chopped	2 medium potatoes, peeled
2 cloves garlic, minced	and diced
½ pound bacon, cut into small	1 package (10 ounces) frozen
pieces	chopped spinach
3 ripe tomatoes, coarsely	1 can (16 ounces) lima beans
chopped	3 carrots, sliced
2 tablespoons chopped	3 stalks celery, chopped
parsley	1 cup elbow macaroni,
½ teaspoon dried basil leaves	cooked and rinsed in
2 teaspoons salt	cold water
½ teaspoon pepper	Grated Romano cheese

Heat the oil in a heavy 8-inch skillet over medium heat. Add the onions, garlic and bacon and cook, stirring, until the onions are transparent. Add the tomatoes, parsley, basil, salt and pepper. Reduce heat and simmer, uncovered, for 20 to 30 minutes or until tomatoes are reduced.

Put the water into a large pot and bring to a boil. Add the tomato mixture and the potatoes, spinach, lima beans, carrots and celery. Simmer for 30 minutes or until the vegetables are tender. Add the pasta a few minutes before serving. Serve hot with grated Romano sprinkled over the top.

4 to 6 servings.

Always slightly under-cook pasta that is to be used in soup. It will continue cooking in the soup and you want it to still be firm when the soup is served.

Ceci Soup with Ditalini

¼ pound salt pork, diced	2 tablespoons tomato paste
2 tablespoons oil	1½ quarts beef broth
2 small onions, coarsely chopped	2 cans (16 ounces each) chick peas
2 cloves garlic, minced	1 cup ditalini, cooked and rinsed in cold water
¼ teaspoon pepper	¼ cup grated Romano or Parmesan cheese
¼ teaspoon dried oregano leaves	
¼ teaspoon dried rosemary leaves	

The chick pea, popular-ized in this country as the "garbanzo," is a staple of the Mediter-ranean. In Italy, it is known as the "ceci."

Heat the salt pork in the oil in a large heavy pot over medium heat until the salt pork begins rendering its fat. Add the onions, garlic, pepper, oregano and rosemary. Cook, stirring, until the onions are transparent. Add the tomato paste and beef broth. Lower heat and simmer, uncovered, for 15 minutes. Add the chick peas with their liquid and the pasta. Continue cooking until the chick peas are heated through. Serve sprinkled with grated cheese.

4 to 6 servings.

Spinach and Bean Minestra

4 tablespoons oil	1 teaspoon salt
½ pound bacon, cut into small pieces	¼ teaspoon pepper
3 cloves garlic, minced	¼ teaspoon dried oregano leaves
1 pound spinach, cooked, drained and chopped (reserve the cooking water)	1 cup ditalini, cooked and rinsed in cold water
	1 can (20 ounces) cannellini
	½ cup grated Romano cheese

Heat the oil in a heavy pot over medium heat. Cook the bacon until it is done but not crisp. Pour off all but about 6 tablespoons of the fat. Add the garlic. Cook, stirring, until golden. Add the spinach and its cooking water, the salt, pepper, oregano, ditalini and can-nellini, liquid and all. Stir over low heat for 5 minutes. Stir in the Romano cheese and serve.

4 servings.

■ Minestra is a very thick soup, almost a stew.

Pizza

Basic Pizza Dough

2 envelopes dry yeast	1½ teaspoons salt
2 cups warm water	½ teaspoon sugar
5 cups all-purpose flour	4 tablespoons oil

Dissolve the yeast in the water. Put the flour into a mixing bowl and stir in the salt and sugar. Make a well in the flour and add the yeast mixture and oil. Mix the flour in until the dough is soft but not sticky. If the dough is sticky, add additional flour during the next step.

Turn the dough out onto a lightly floured board. (If the dough is sticky, use more flour.) Knead for about 10 minutes or until the dough is smooth and elastic. (The dough will pop back if you stick a finger into it.)

Put the dough in a lightly oiled bowl and brush it with oil. Cover with a towel and put in a warm place. Allow to rise for 1½ to 2 hours or until the dough is doubled in size. (A hole remains if you poke your finger into the dough.)

Remove the dough from the bowl and punch it down on a board. Divide into 2 equal balls, cover and let rest for 10 minutes. Taking 1 ball at a time, roll it out or pat and stretch it into a circle about 14 inches in diameter. The dough should be thinner at the center than at the edge. Pinch the edge of the dough up to form a rim and place the whole on a lightly oiled baking sheet. Prick lightly all over with a fork.

Fill the circles (see page 60 for suggestions) with the filling of your choice and bake in a preheated 400° oven for about 30 minutes or until the crust is done.

Makes enough dough for two 13-inch pizzas.

Don't make a federal case out of using yeast. The only things that kill it are time and heat. The water you dissolve it in should be between 105° and 115°. You don't need a thermometer. Just make sure the water isn't hot.

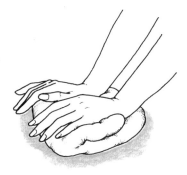

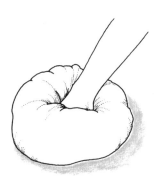

Well-kneaded dough pops back when you stick a finger into it. Dough that's risen enough doesn't pop back at all. The hole stays.

Rye Pizza Dough

2	envelopes dry yeast	3	tablespoons caraway seed
2	cups warm water	1½	teaspoons salt
3	cups all-purpose flour	½	teaspoon sugar
2	cups rye flour	4	tablespoons oil

Dissolve the yeast in the water. Put the flours into a mixing bowl and stir in the caraway seed, salt and sugar. Make a well in the flour and add the yeast mixture and oil. Mix the flour in until the dough is soft but not sticky. If the dough is sticky, add additional flour during the next step.

Turn the dough out onto a lightly floured board. (If the dough is sticky, use more flour.) Knead for about 10 minutes or until the dough is smooth and elastic.

Put the dough in a lightly oiled bowl and brush it with oil. Cover with a towel and put in a warm place. Allow to rise for 1½ to 2 hours or until the dough is doubled in size.

Remove the dough from the bowl and punch it down on a board. Divide it into 2 equal balls, cover and let rest for 10 minutes. Taking 1 ball at a time, roll it out or pat and stretch it into a circle about 14 inches in diameter. The dough should be thinner at the center than at the edge. Pinch the edge of the dough up to form a rim and place the whole on a lightly oiled baking sheet. Prick lightly all over with a fork.

Fill (see page 60 for suggestions) with the filling of your choice and bake in a preheated 400° oven for about 30 minutes or until the crust is done.

Makes enough dough for two 13-inch pizzas.

Whole Wheat Pizza Dough

2	envelopes dry yeast	1½	teaspoons salt
2	cups warm water	½	teaspoon sugar
2	cups all-purpose flour	½	cup oil
3	cups whole wheat flour		

Dissolve the yeast in the water. Put the flours into a mixing bowl and stir in the salt and sugar. Make a well in the flour and add the yeast mixture and oil. Mix the flour in until the dough is soft but not sticky. If the dough is sticky, add additional flour during the next step.

Turn the dough out onto a lightly floured board. (If the dough is sticky, use more flour.) Knead for about 10 minutes or until the dough is smooth and elastic.

Put the dough in a lightly oiled bowl and brush it with oil. Cover with a towel and put in a warm place. Allow to rise for 1½ to 2 hours or until the dough is doubled in size.

Remove the dough from the bowl and punch it down on a board. Divide it into 2 equal balls, cover and let rest for 10 minutes. Taking 1 ball at a time, roll it out or pat and stretch it into a circle about 14 inches in diameter. The dough should be thinner at the center than at the edge. Pinch the edge of the dough up to form a rim and place the whole on a lightly oiled baking sheet. Prick lightly all over with a fork. Fill (see page 60 for suggestions) with the filling of your choice and bake in a preheated 400° oven for about 30 minutes or until the crust is done.

Makes enough dough for two 13-inch pizzas.

Pizza dough makes good bread, too. After you've punched it down, shape the dough into 2 loaves and put into greased 8½x4½x2½-inch pans. Let the dough rise again and bake in a preheated 400° oven for 45 to 50 minutes or until the loaves sound hollow when tapped. Remove from the pans and cool on a rack.

Ricotta and Dill Pizza Dough

2 envelopes dry yeast	1 teaspoon sugar
½ cup warm water	¼ teaspoon baking soda
1 cup ricotta cheese, heated until just warm	2 teaspoons dill seed
	1 tablespoon butter, melted
1 teaspoon salt	2 eggs, beaten
¼ teaspoon pepper	3 cups all-purpose flour

Dissolve the yeast in the water. Put the ricotta into a large mixing bowl and add the yeast mixture. Beat in the salt, pepper, sugar, baking soda, dill seed, melted butter and eggs until all are well combined. Stir in 2 cups of the flour. Add the remaining flour gradually until the dough is soft but not sticky.

Turn the dough out onto a lightly floured board. Knead for about 10 minutes or until the dough is smooth and elastic.

Put the dough in a lightly oiled bowl and brush with oil. Cover with a towel and put in a warm place. Allow to rise for 1½ to 2 hours or until the dough is doubled in size.

Remove the dough from the bowl and punch it down on a board. Divide it into 2 equal balls, cover and let rest for 10 minutes. Taking one ball at a time, roll it out or pat and stretch it into a circle about 14 inches in diameter. The dough should be thinner at the center than at the edge. Pinch the edge of the dough up to form a rim and place the whole on a lightly oiled baking sheet. Prick lightly all over with a fork.

Fill (see page 60 for suggestions) with the filling of your choice and bake in a preheated 400° oven for about 30 minutes or until the crust is done.

Makes enough dough for two 13-inch pizzas.

Assembling Pizzas

Two 13-inch unbaked pizzas made with the dough of your choice (pages 57-59)
2 tablespoons oil

1 recipe Pizza Sauce (below)
½ cup grated Romano cheese Filling (below)
¾ pound mozzarella cheese, shredded or thinly sliced

Place the pizzas on 2 lightly oiled baking sheets. Brush with the oil and cover with the sauce. Sprinkle with the Romano cheese and add the filling. Sprinkle with the mozzarella and bake in a preheated 400° oven for 30 minutes or until the crust is done.

Pizza Sauce

1 can (29 ounces) tomato puree
4 tablespoons oil
1 teaspoon salt

¼ teaspoon pepper
¼ teaspoon dried oregano leaves
¼ teaspoon garlic powder

Combine all ingredients in a pot. Simmer gently, uncovered, for about 30 minutes.

Makes about 3 cups.

Filling

☐ 1 can (2 ounces) anchovy fillets
☐ ½ pound mushrooms, sliced
☐ 1 pound Italian sausage, fried and sliced
☐ 1 pound ground beef, cooked until browned

☐ 4 large onions, thinly sliced
☐ ½ pound pepperoni, thinly sliced
☐ 1 large green pepper, seeded and cut lengthwise into slivers

Any one of these ingredients alone is sufficient in quantity to fill two 13-inch circles. Combine or use separately as you wish. Garnish with pitted black or green olives or stuffed green olives.

Pizza with Garlic and Oil

½ recipe Basic Pizza Dough (page 57)
4 tablespoons olive oil

2 tablespoons minced garlic
¼ teaspoon dried oregano leaves

Prepare and roll out the pizza dough as directed for two 13-inch pizzas, but make it much thinner than a regular pizza. Place on a lightly oiled baking sheet. Brush the olive oil over the surface. Sprinkle with the garlic and oregano.

Bake in a preheated 400° oven for 15 to 20 minutes or until the garlic is browned and the dough crispy. The crust should be done almost to the point of burning.

Makes two 13-inch pizzas.

■ This is the original pizza before it got dressed up by Americans. You can sprinkle ½ cup of grated Romano cheese on top before baking if you want to add a little something extra.

Pizza Within a Pizza

1 recipe Pizza Sauce (page 60)	½ teaspoon garlic powder
1 envelope dry yeast	½ pound bulk sausage, fried and drained
1 cup warm water	¼ cup grated Romano cheese
3 cups all-purpose flour	1 small onion, finely chopped
1 teaspoon salt	2 tablespoons oil
1 teaspoon sugar	
½ teaspoon pepper	½ cup grated Romano cheese
¼ teaspoon dried oregano leaves	1½ cups shredded mozzarella cheese

Prepare the sauce. Dissolve the yeast in the water. Put the flour into a mixing bowl and stir in the salt, sugar, pepper, oregano and garlic powder. Add the sausage, ¼ cup grated Romano and the onion. Mix together. Make a well in the flour mixture and add the yeast mixture, the oil and ¼ cup Pizza Sauce. Mix in the flour until the dough is soft but not sticky. If the dough is sticky, add additional flour during the next step.

Turn the dough out onto a lightly floured board. (If the dough is sticky, use more flour.) Knead for about 10 minutes or until the dough is smooth and elastic. Put the dough in a lightly oiled bowl and brush it with oil. Cover with a towel and put in a warm place. Allow to rise for 1½ to 2 hours or until the dough is doubled in size.

Remove the dough from the bowl and punch in down on a board. Divide it into 2 equal balls, cover and let rest for 10 minutes. Taking 1 ball at a time, roll it out or pat and stretch it into a circle about 14 inches in diameter. The dough should be thinner at the center than at the edge. Pinch the edge of the dough up to form a rim and place the whole on a lightly oiled baking sheet. Prick lightly all over with a fork.

Divide the remaining sauce between the two pizzas. Sprinkle each with 4 tablespoons grated Romano cheese and ¾ cup shredded mozzarella. Bake in a preheated 400° oven for about 30 minutes or until the crust is done.

Makes two 13-inch pizzas.

You can make a big hit at your next party with little 3- to 4-inch pizzas. Prepare and fill them the same way you do big pizzas. Bake them on a greased sheet at 400° for 12 to 15 minutes.

"My" Calzone

> If my servings are large, it's because food means love. Don't stint on either.

½ recipe Basic Pizza Dough (page 57)
½ pound sweet or hot Italian sausage
4 tablespoons oil
2 small onions, finely chopped
2 cloves garlic, minced

6 cups ricotta cheese
3 eggs, beaten
½ cup grated Romano cheese
1 teaspoon salt
¼ teaspoon pepper
¼ teaspoon garlic powder
2 teaspoons chopped parsley

Prepare the dough. While it is rising, place the sausage in a shallow baking pan and bake in a 375° oven for 40 minutes or until the sausage is browned and cooked through. Turn once. Cut into ¼-inch slices.

Heat the oil in a heavy skillet over medium heat. Add the onions and garlic. Cook, stirring occasionally, until the onions are transparent. Place in a mixing bowl. Add the sausage, ricotta and remaining ingredients. Mix well.

Divide the risen dough into 2 balls and let rest, covered, for 10 minutes. Roll or pat and stretch 1 of the balls into a square large enough to line a lightly oiled 9x9x2-inch pan.

Add the filling. Roll the remaining dough into a square large enough to cover the filling. Pinch and seal the edges. Cut small slots in the top and brush with 1 egg beaten with 1 teaspoon water. Bake in a preheated 400° oven for about 45 minutes or until the crust is done. Serve hot or cold.

6 servings.

■ This is my way of making calzone. The more traditional method of preparation is to place the filling on one side of the rolled-out pizza and fold the other side over to form a half-moon. Brush lightly with oil and cut slits into the top. Seal the edges and place the pie on a greased baking sheet. Bake in a preheated 400° oven for about 20 minutes or until the crust is done. Halve the recipe for Basic Pizza Dough (page 57) to make 2 calzone.